Hot Shots

Hot Shots * Photographs by Norman Seeff * Flash Books * New York * London

To Bob Cato for the beginning, to Herb Wise for the realization, and love and thanks to Wally, Desiree, Kendrew, Kathy, Faybeth, Peri and Lee.
 Printed in U.S.A. Library of congress catalogue card number: 74-80024. International standard book number: 0-8256-3903-4. Distributed by Quick Fox, 33 West 60th Street, New York 10023

Hot Shots

The photographic session
is a relationship between people,
working together, playing together, making contact;
then the formality of being photographed falls away.
The photograph becomes, not a picture the
eye sees, but an experience of who we are and
what we create together.
Behind the illusion, behind the fantasy
of the public image,
we all love, hate, fear, become children, become serious.
We are all the same.
The camera records the moment in the continuity.
If the moment is real there is no unsureness.
If we leave behind our desires,
the anxiety of our needs, the subjectivity of ego;
if we still our thoughts,
the veil which obscures the essence is lifted
and we are open,
able to see, listen, make contact ......
We are on the same journey together.

N. S.

New York June 1974

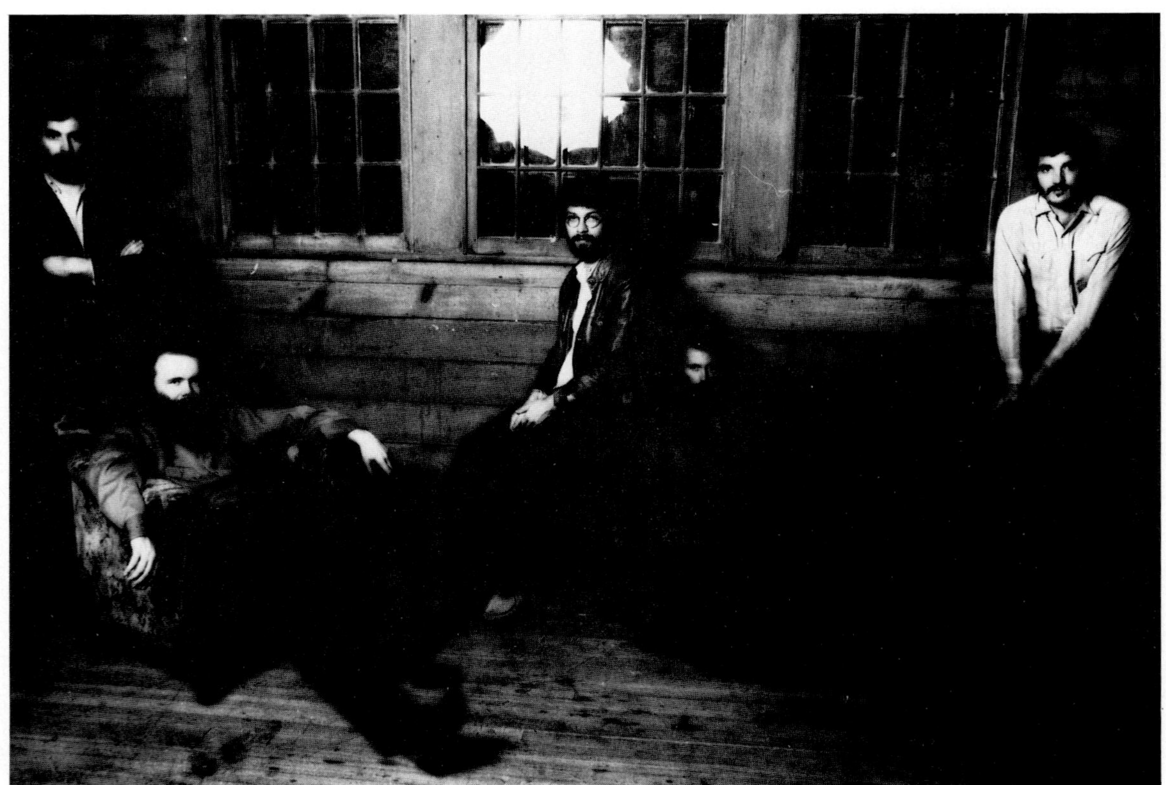

1

2

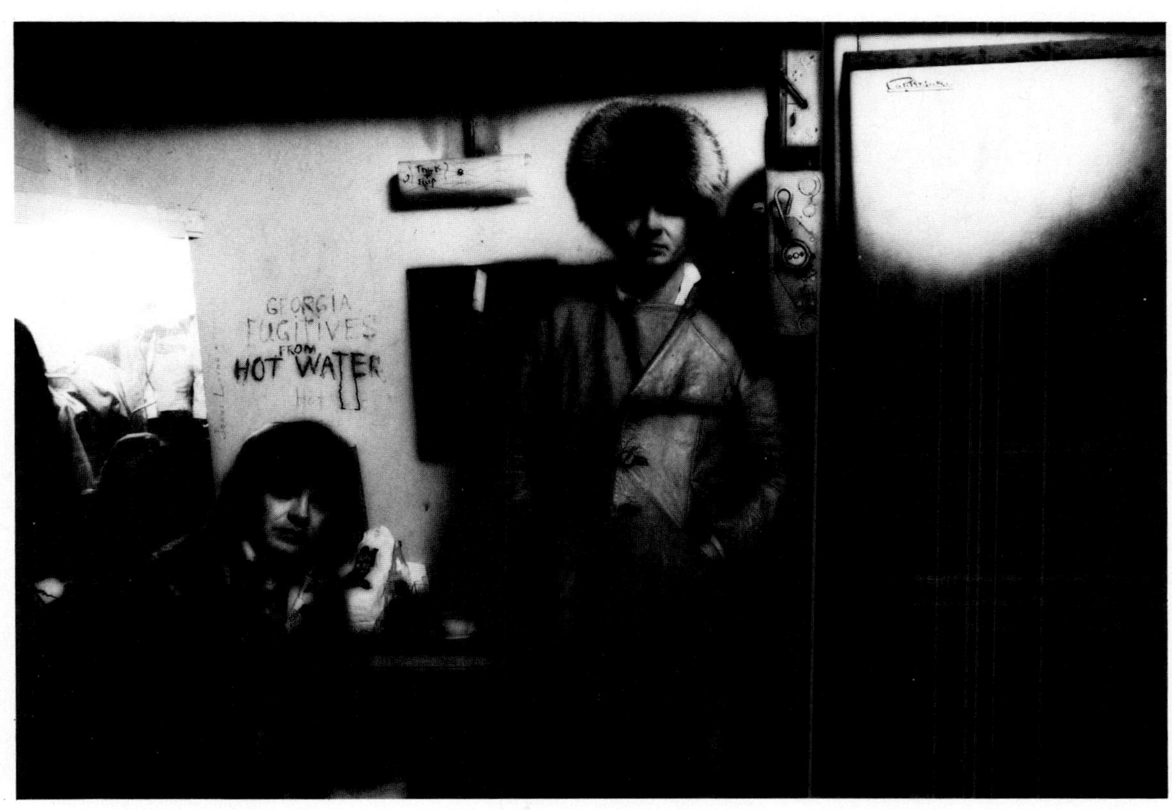

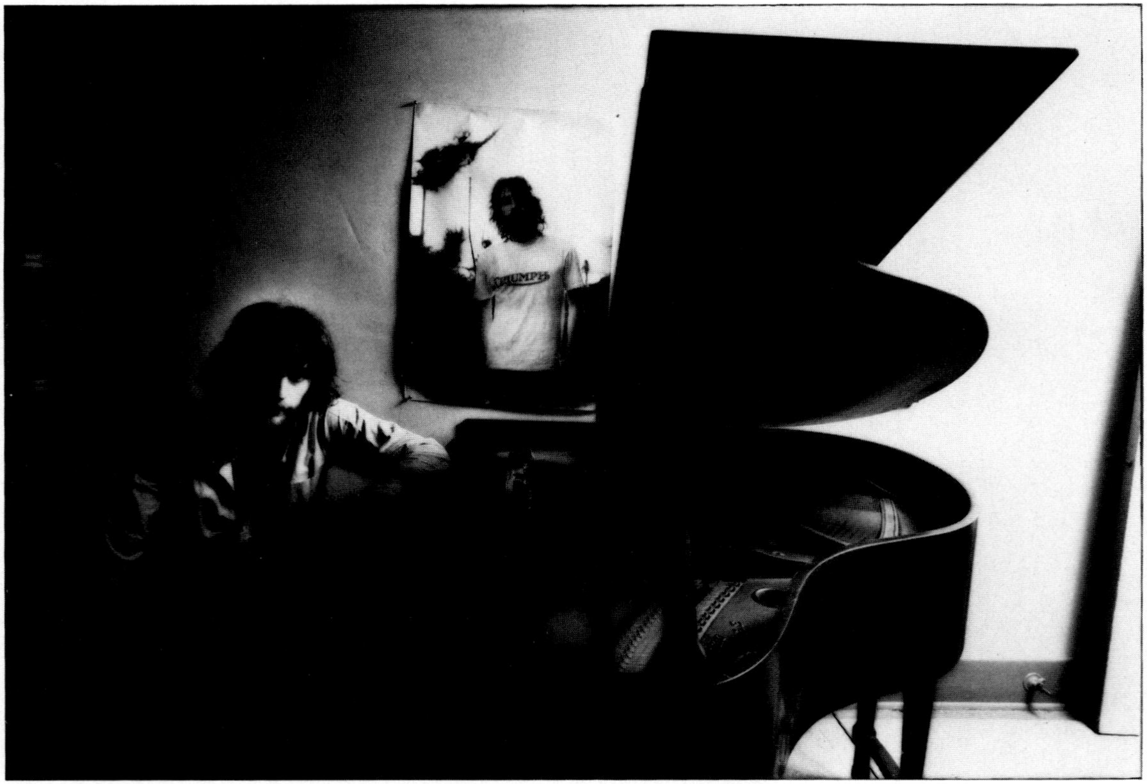

3

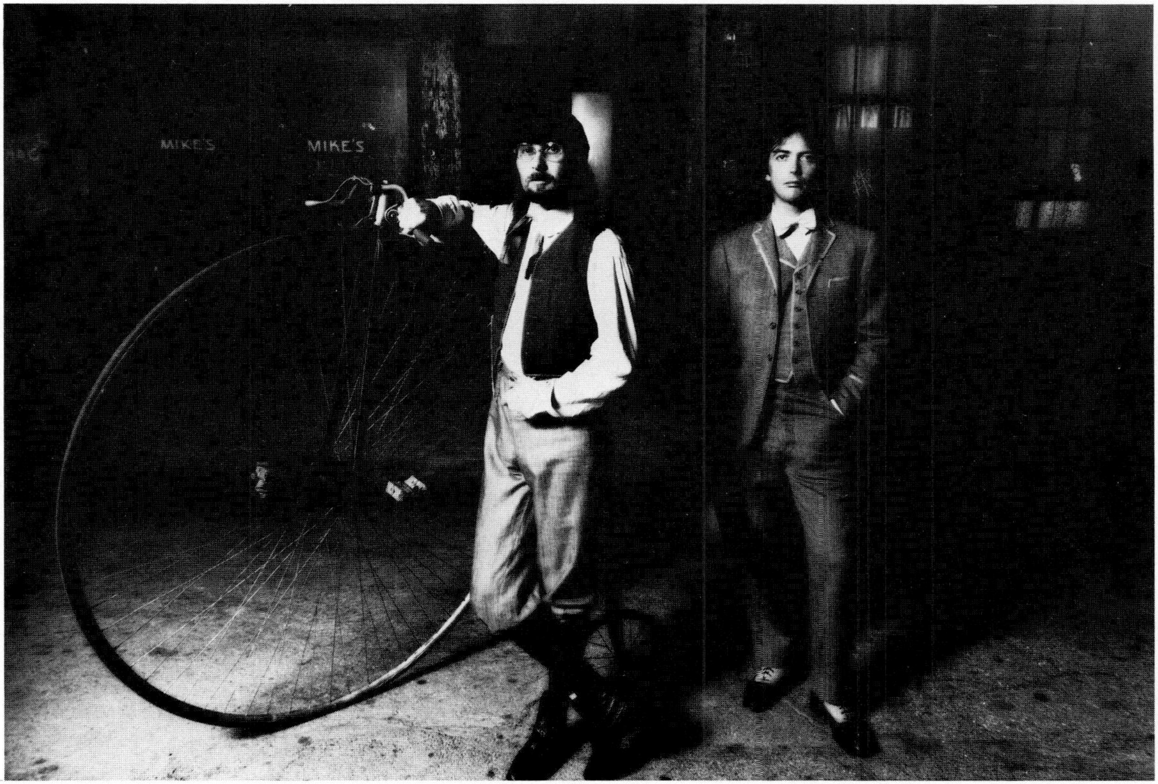

4

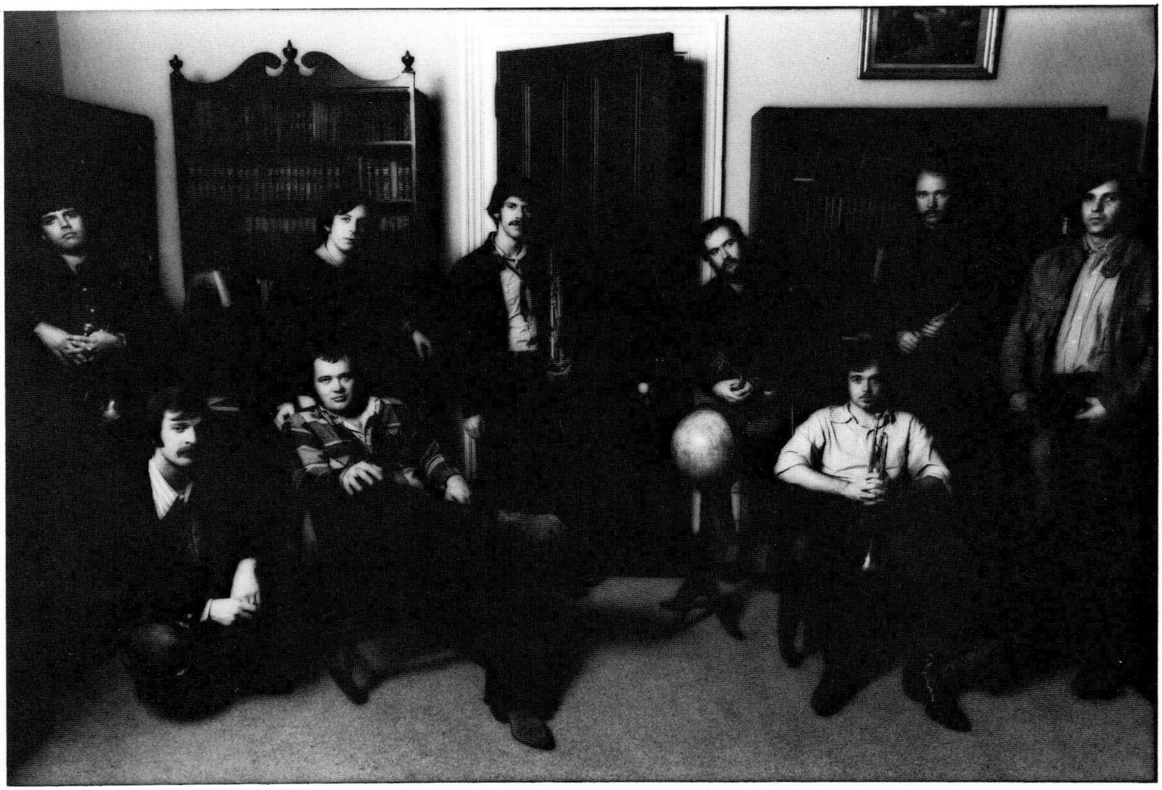

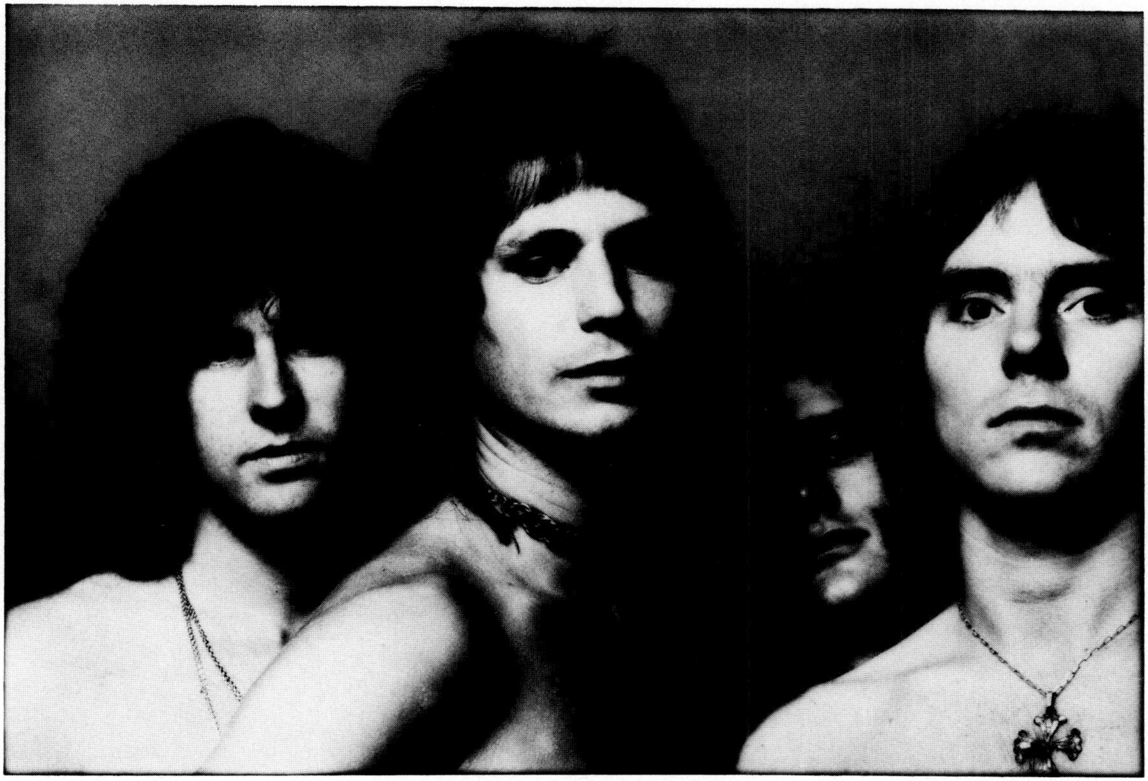

6

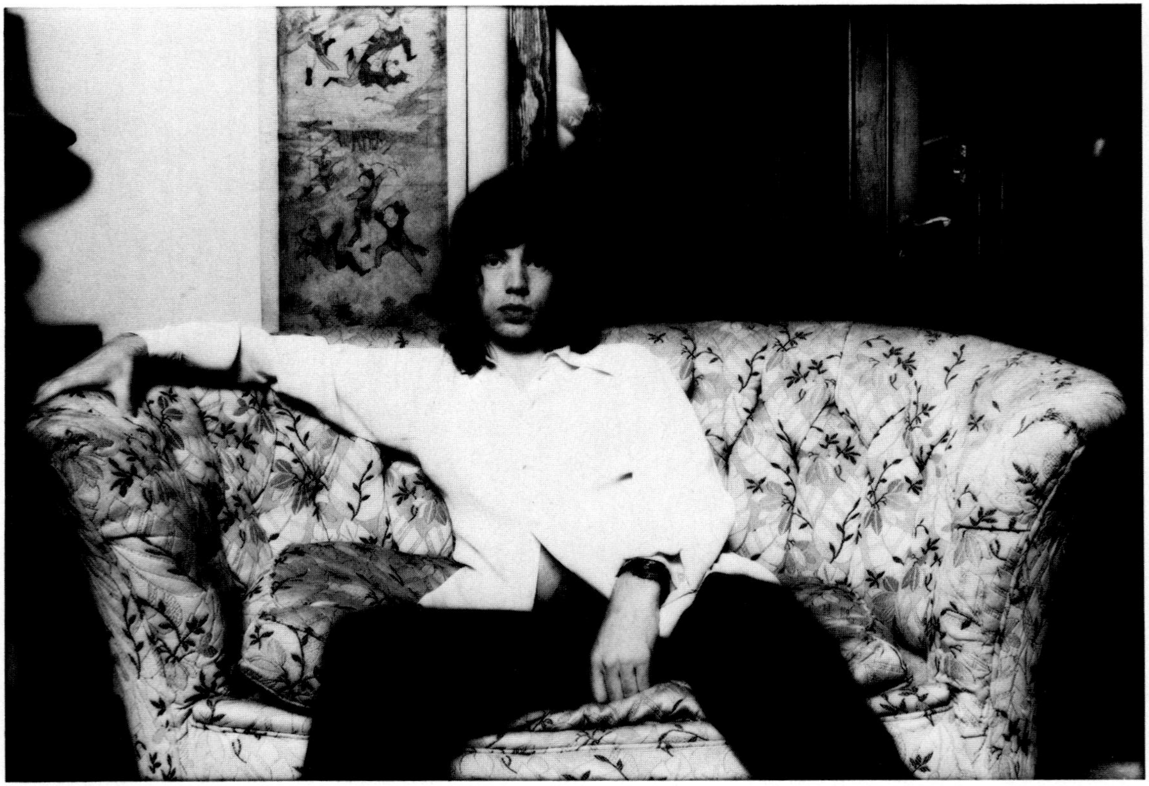

7

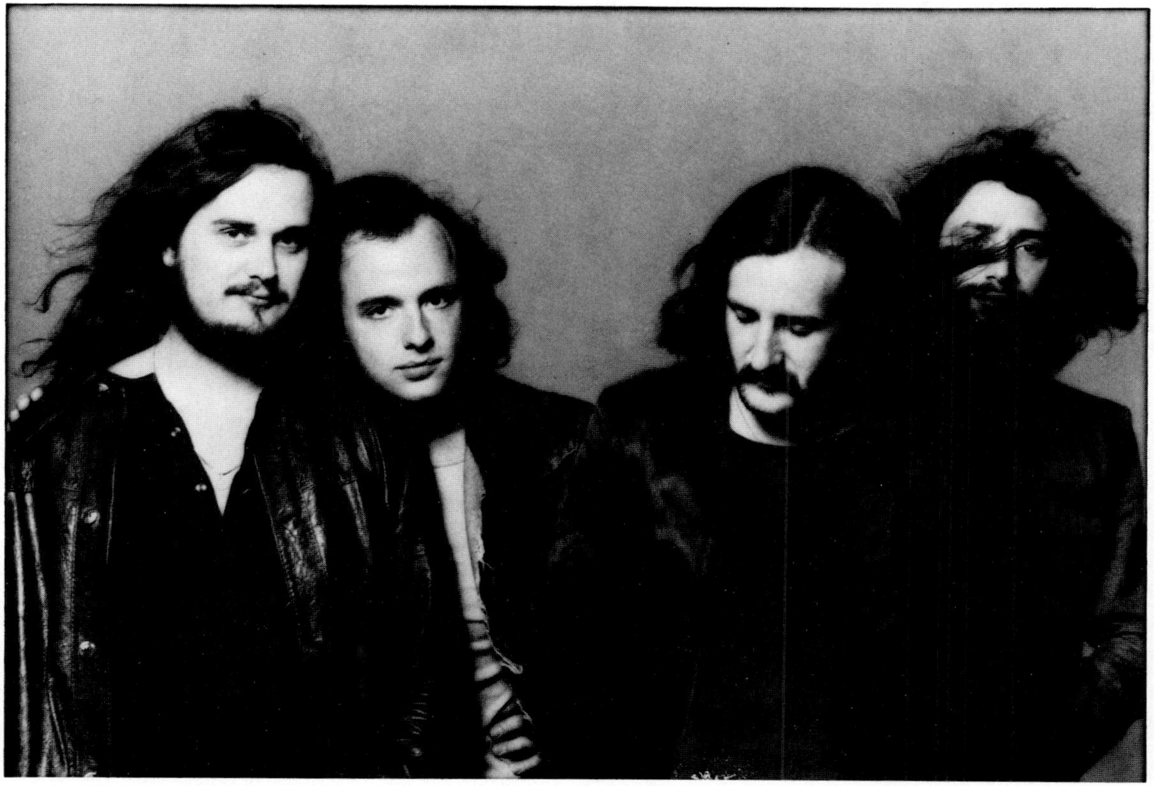

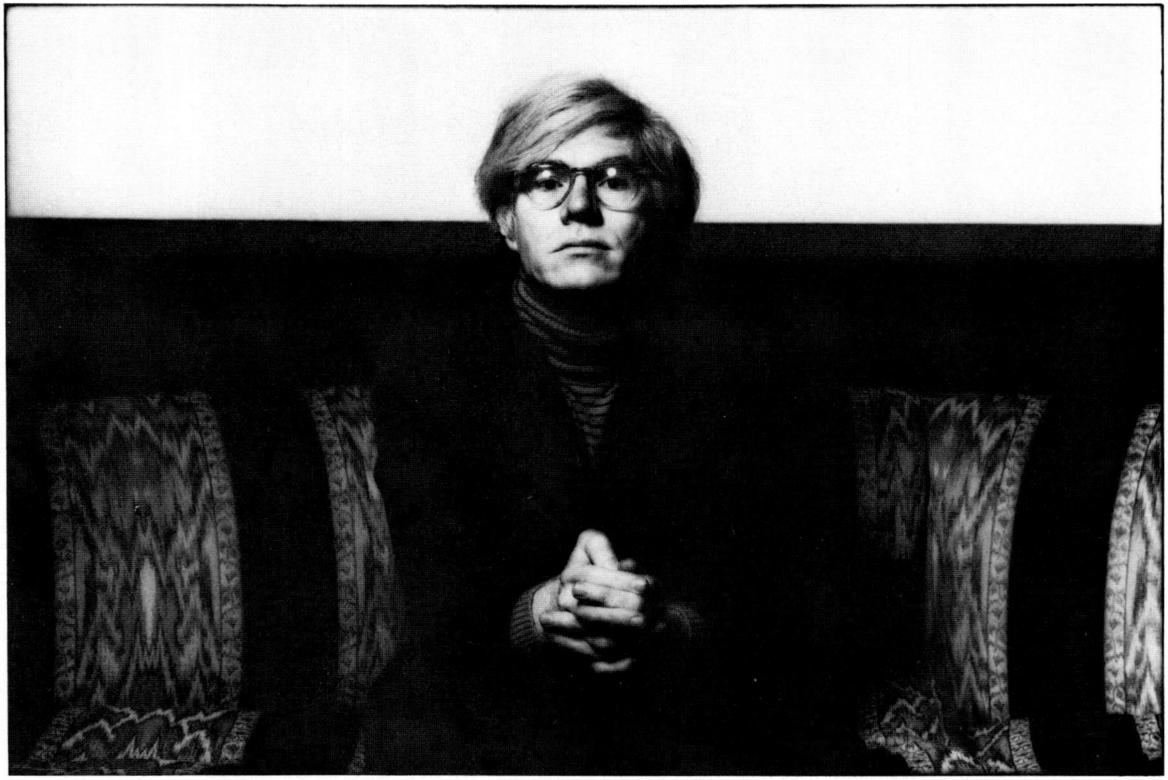

9

10

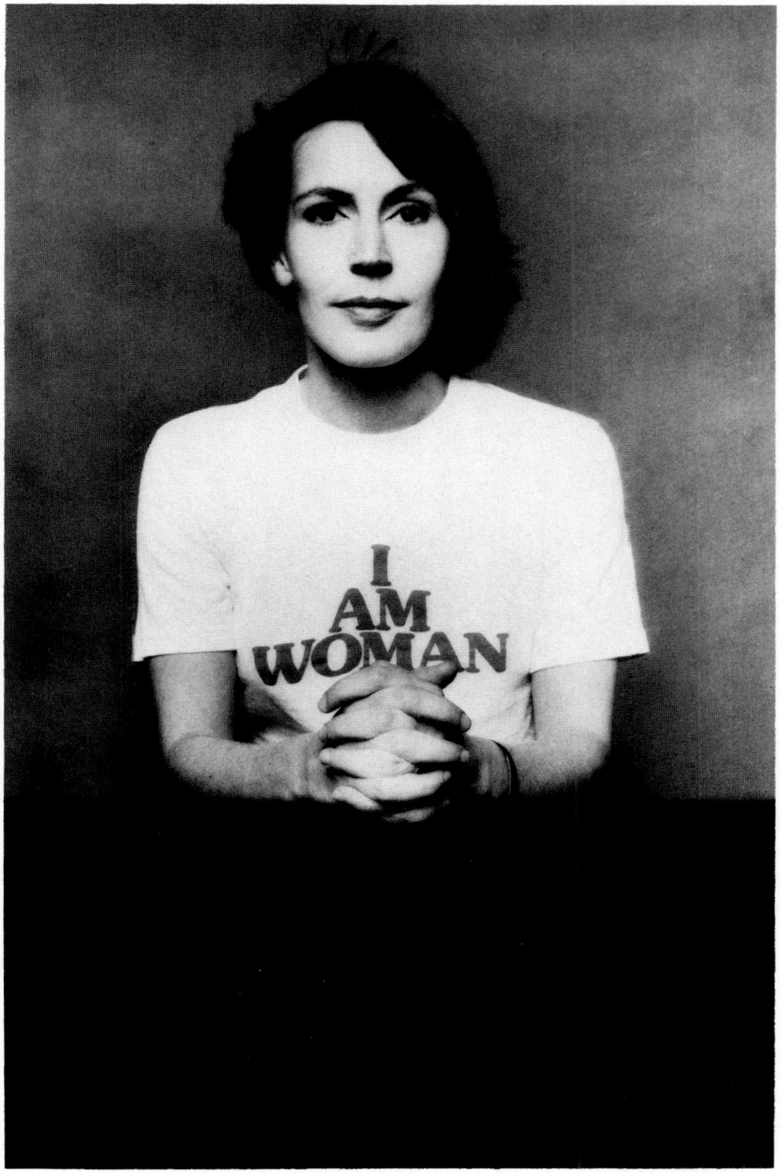

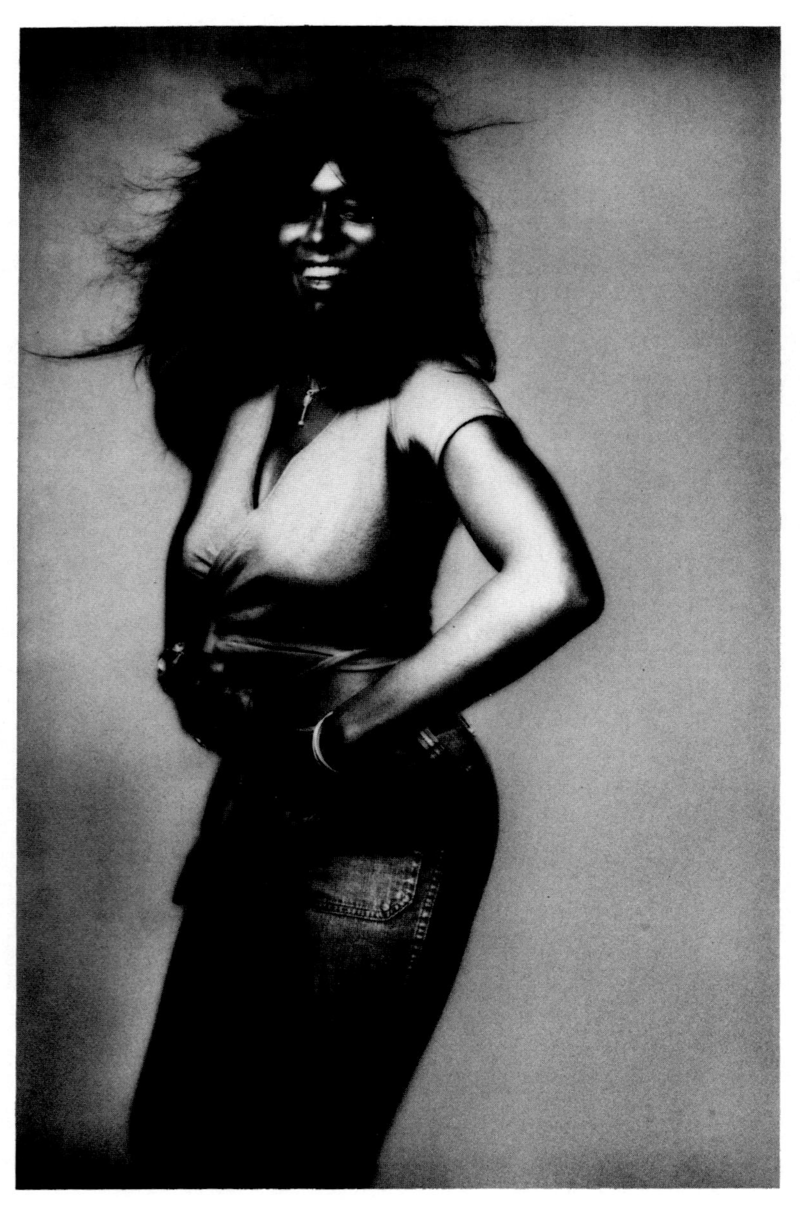

12

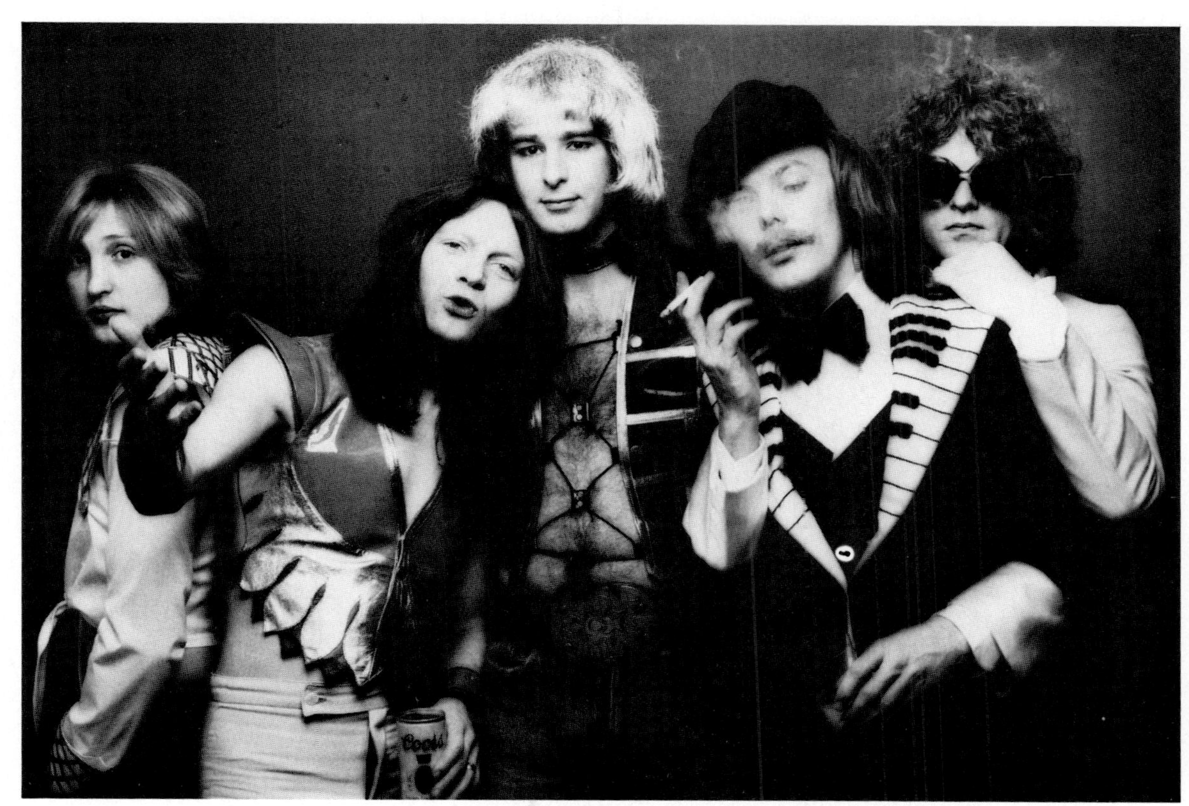

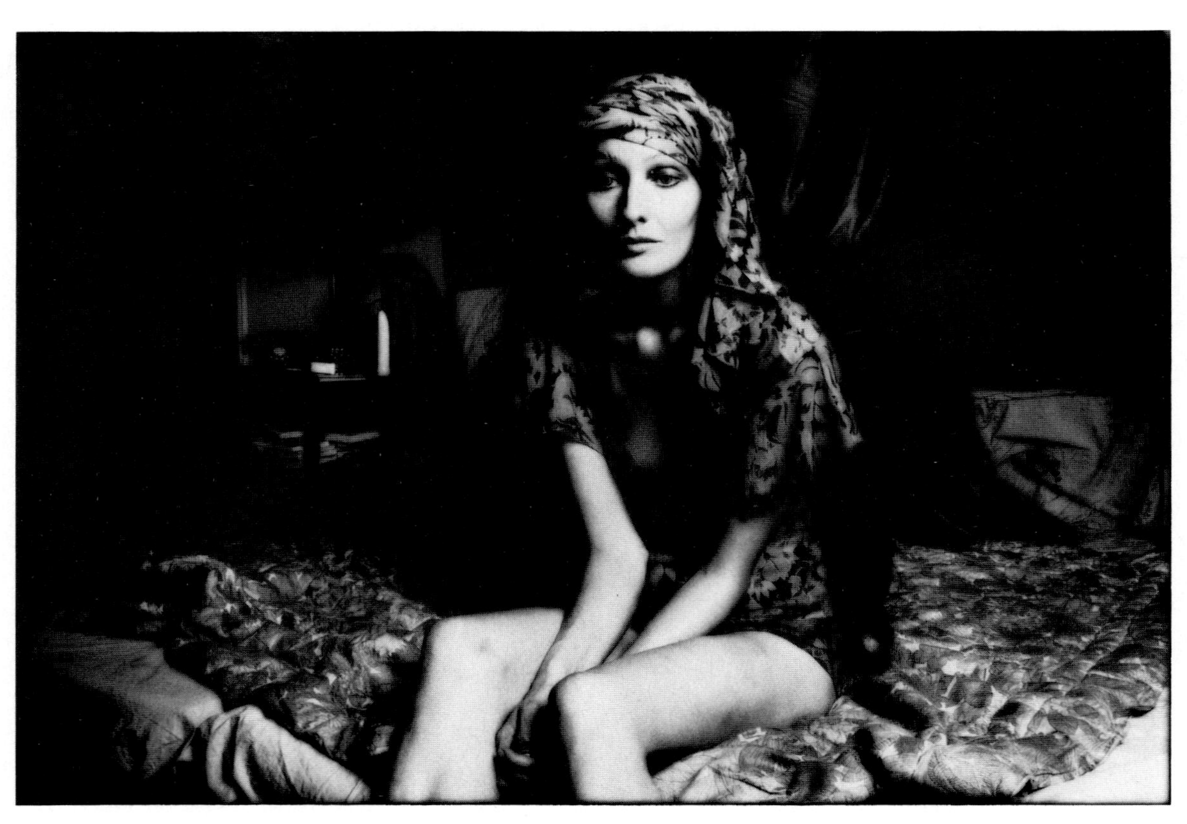

13

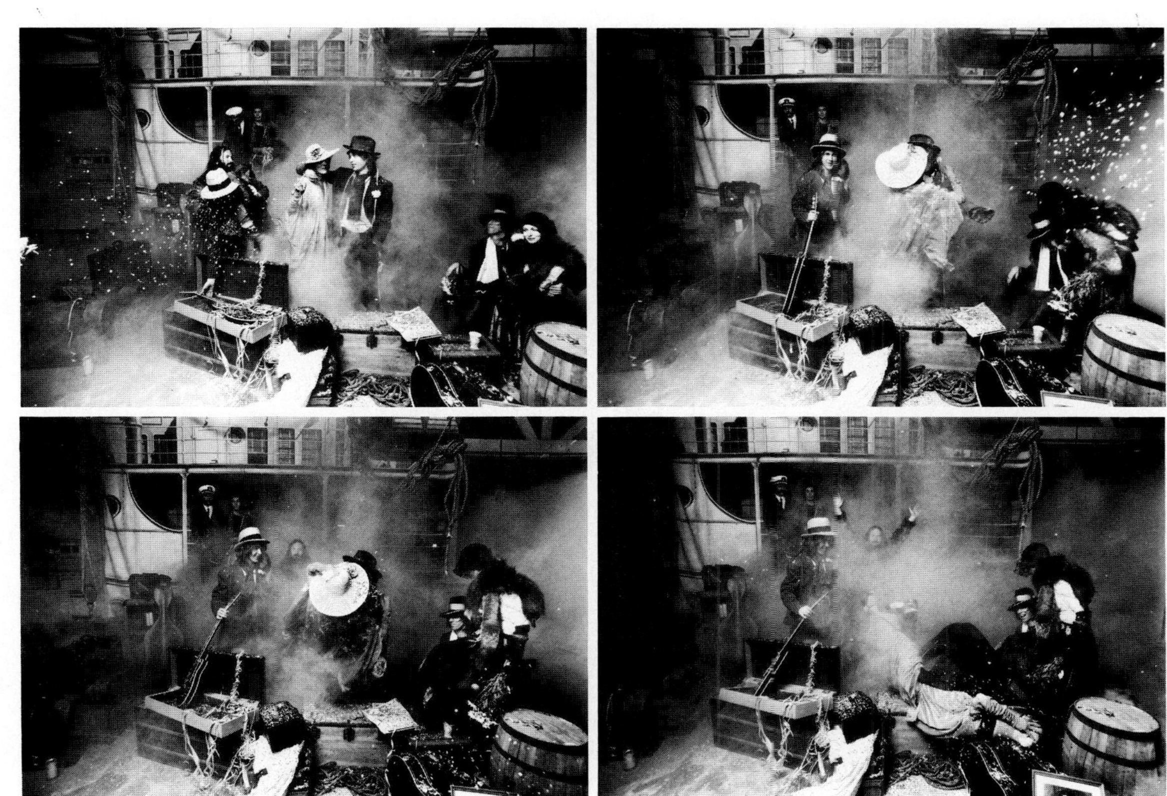

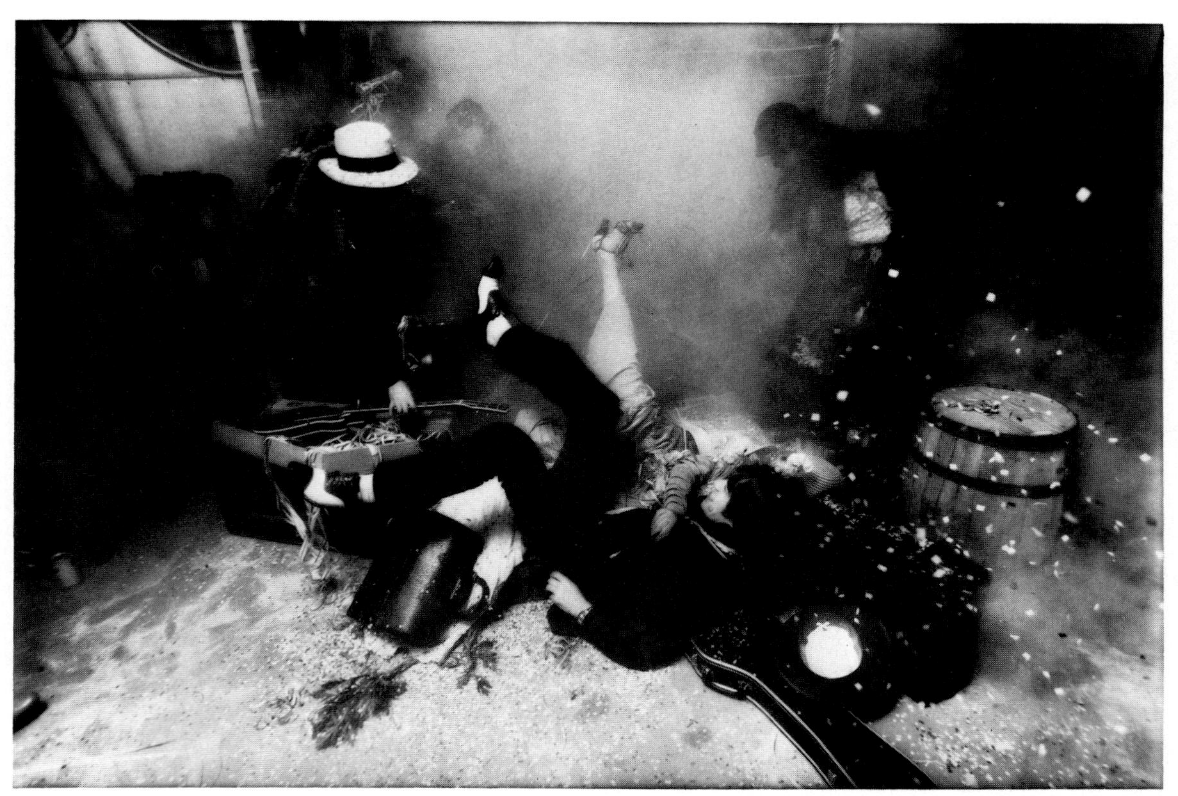

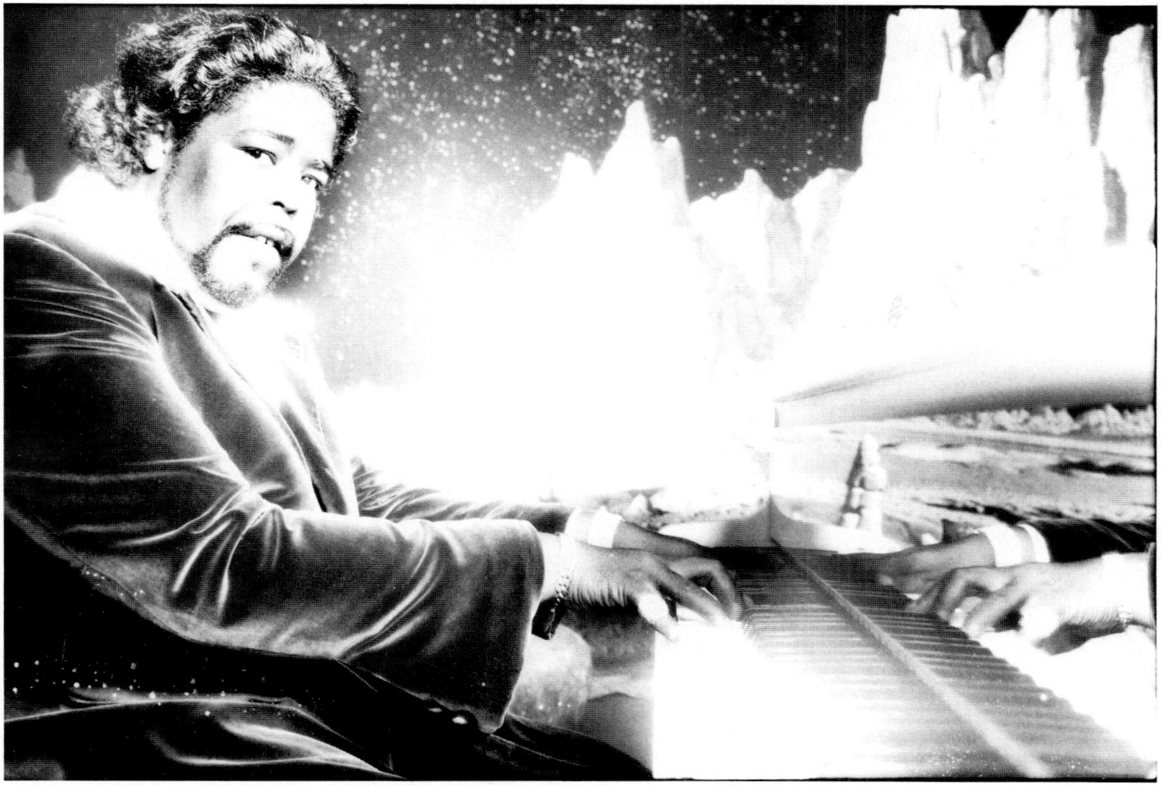

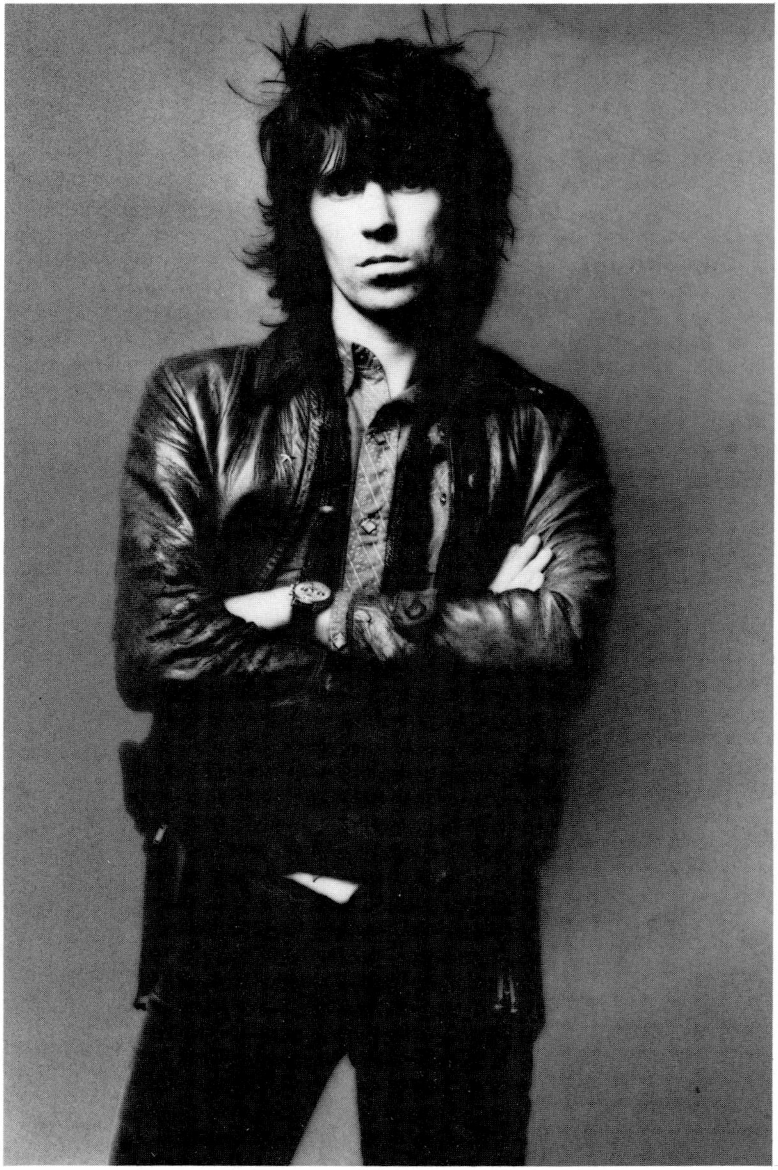

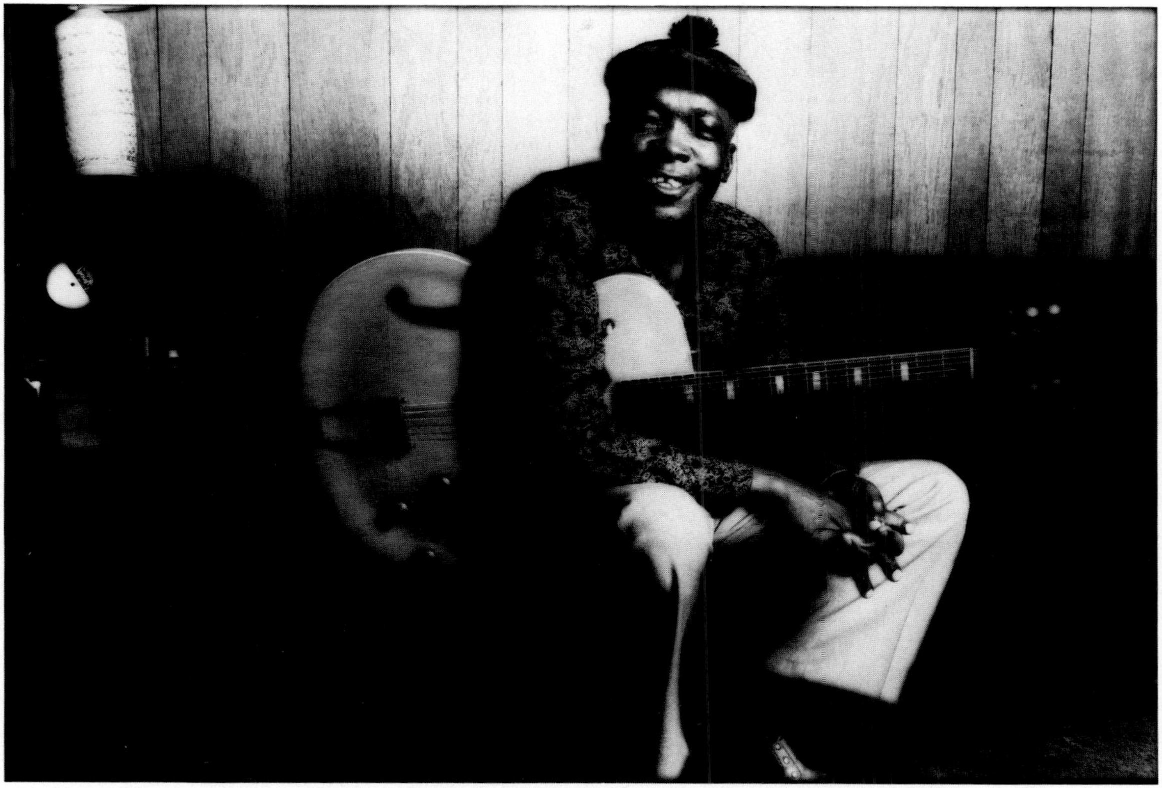

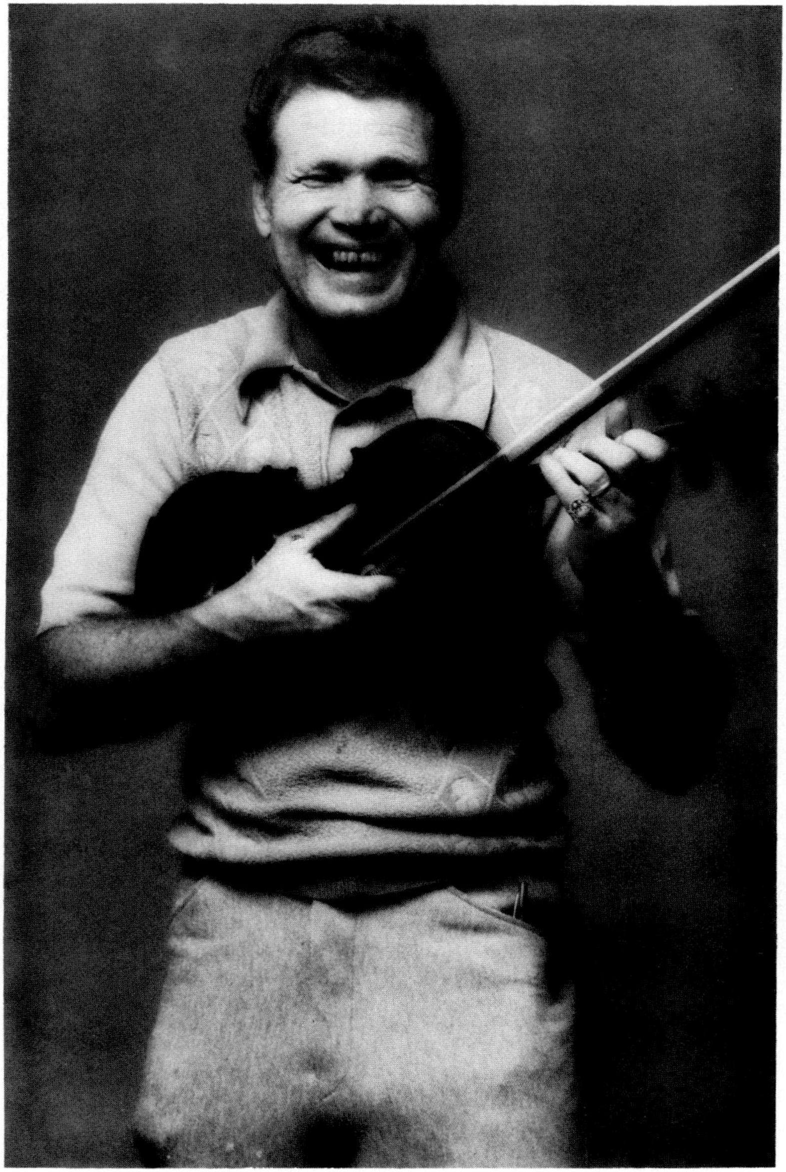

20

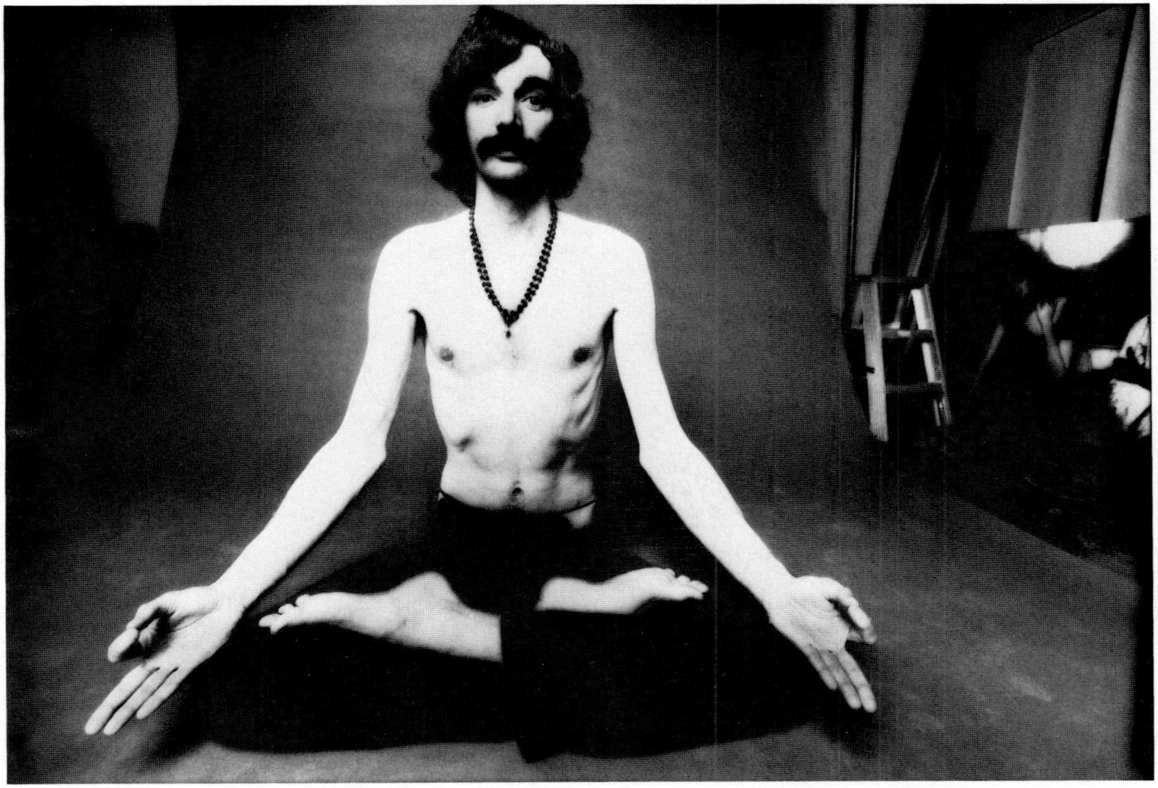

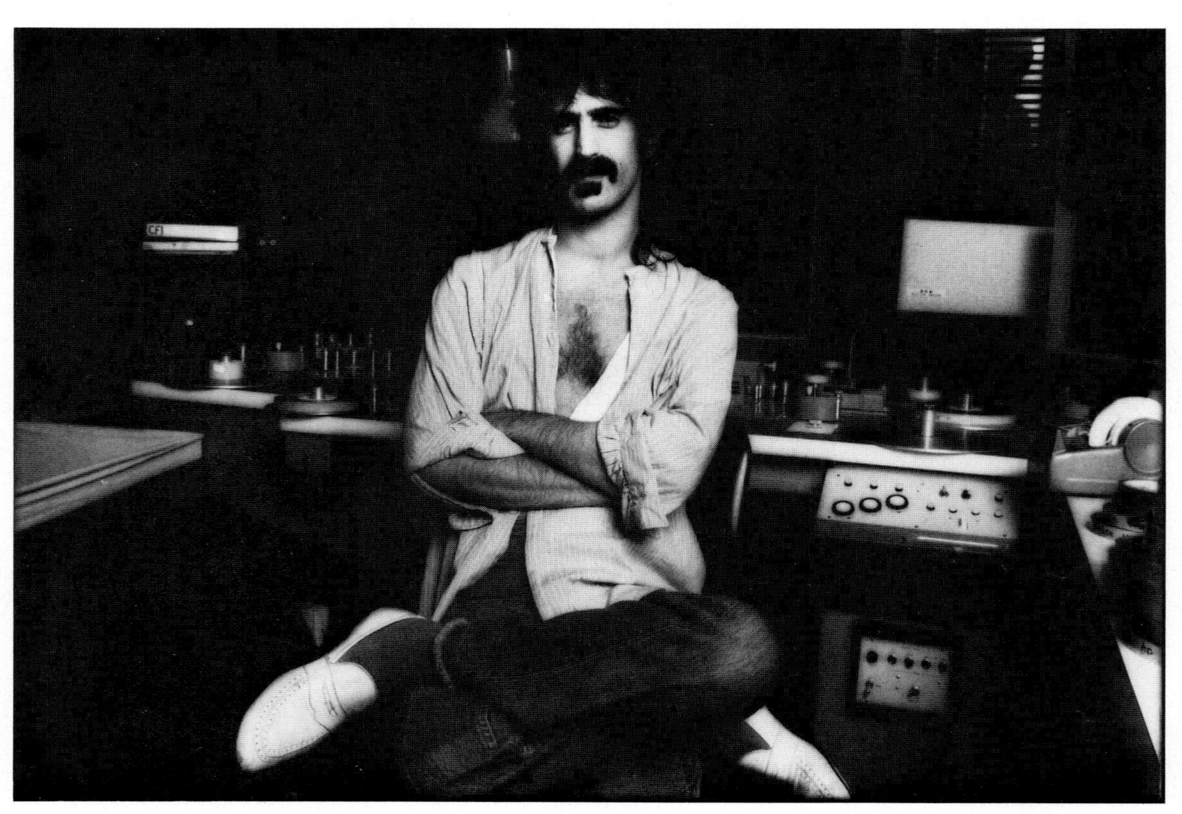

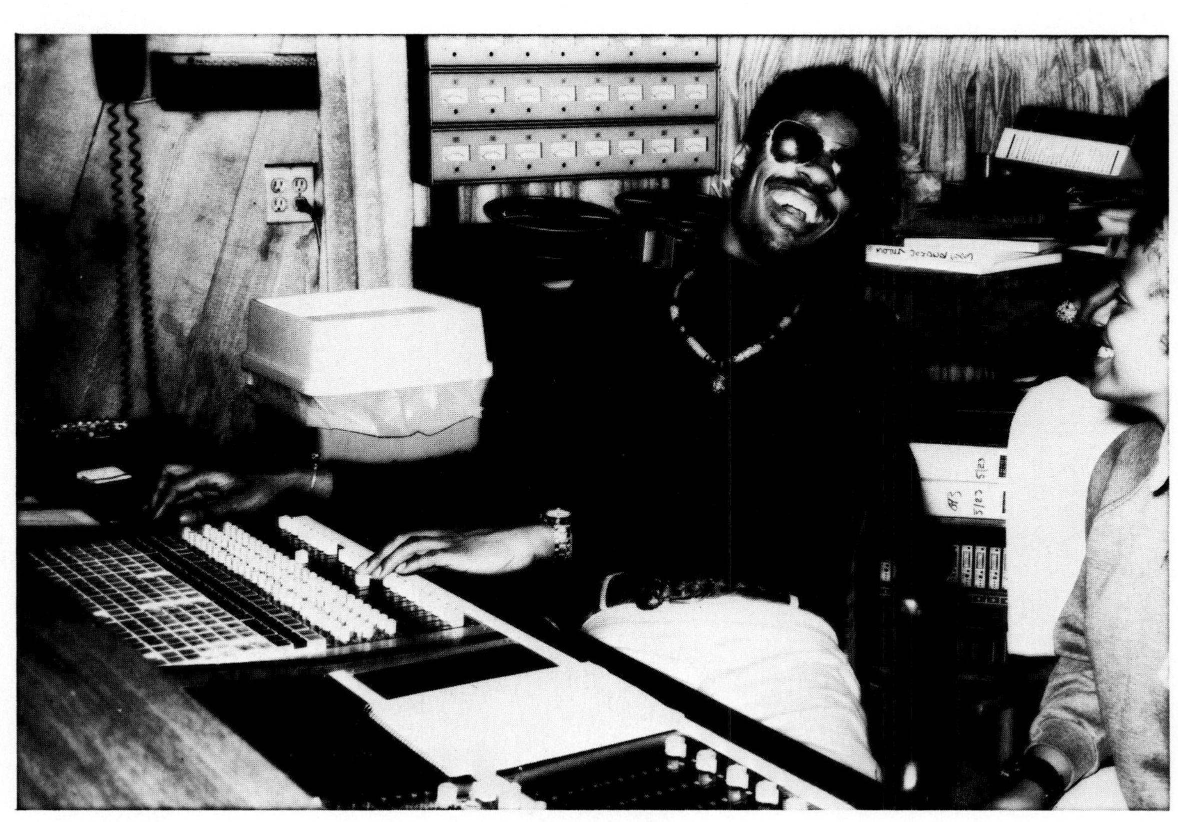

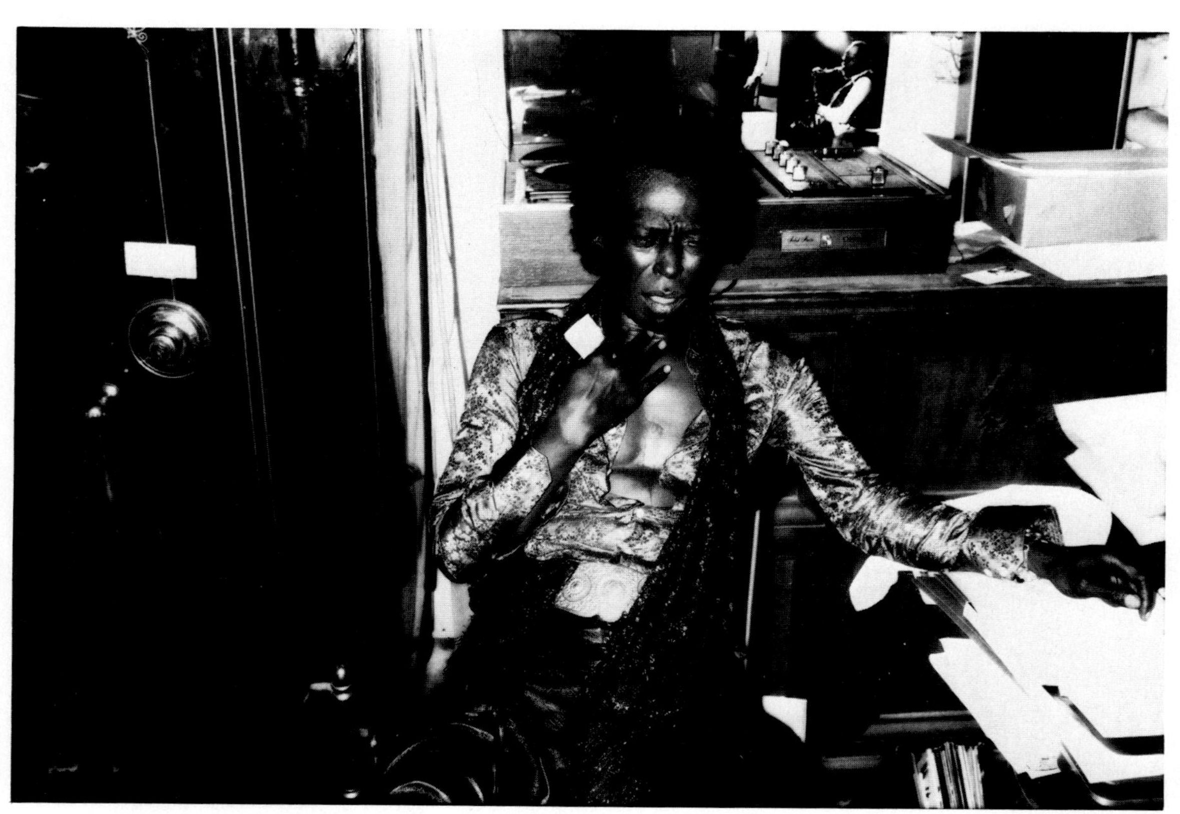

24

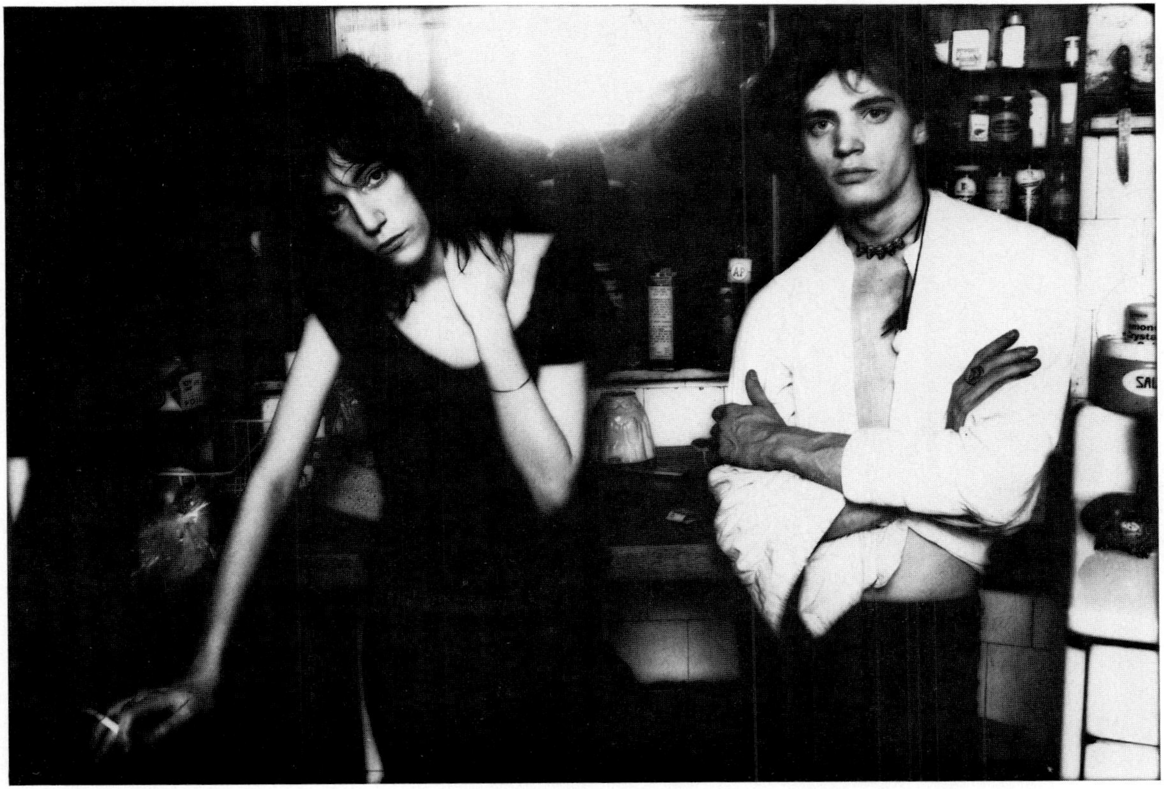

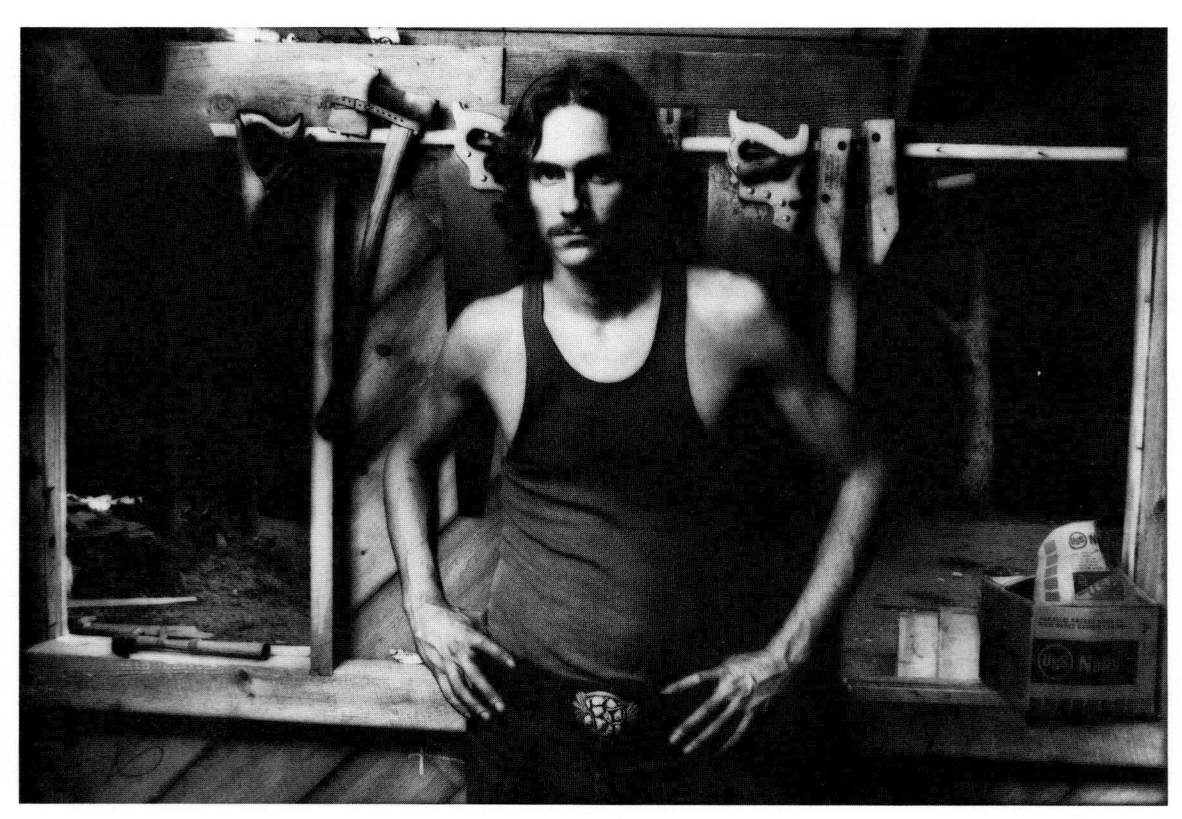

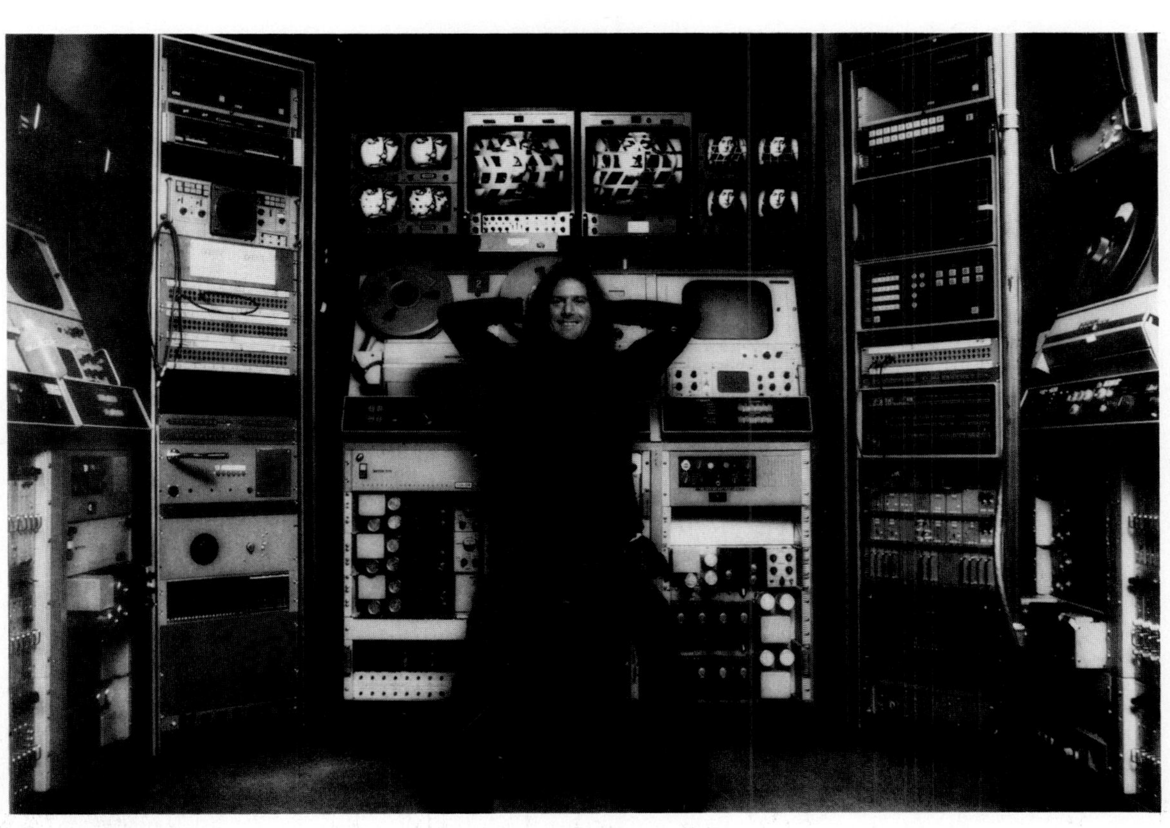

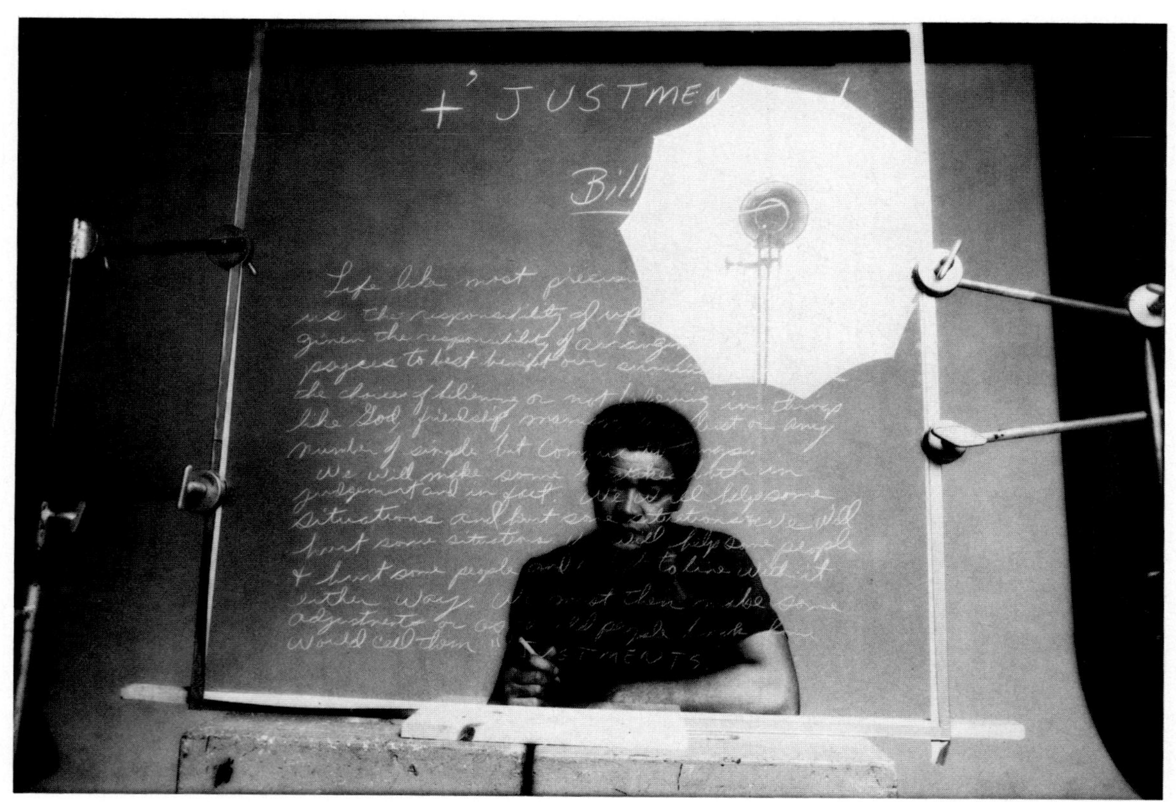

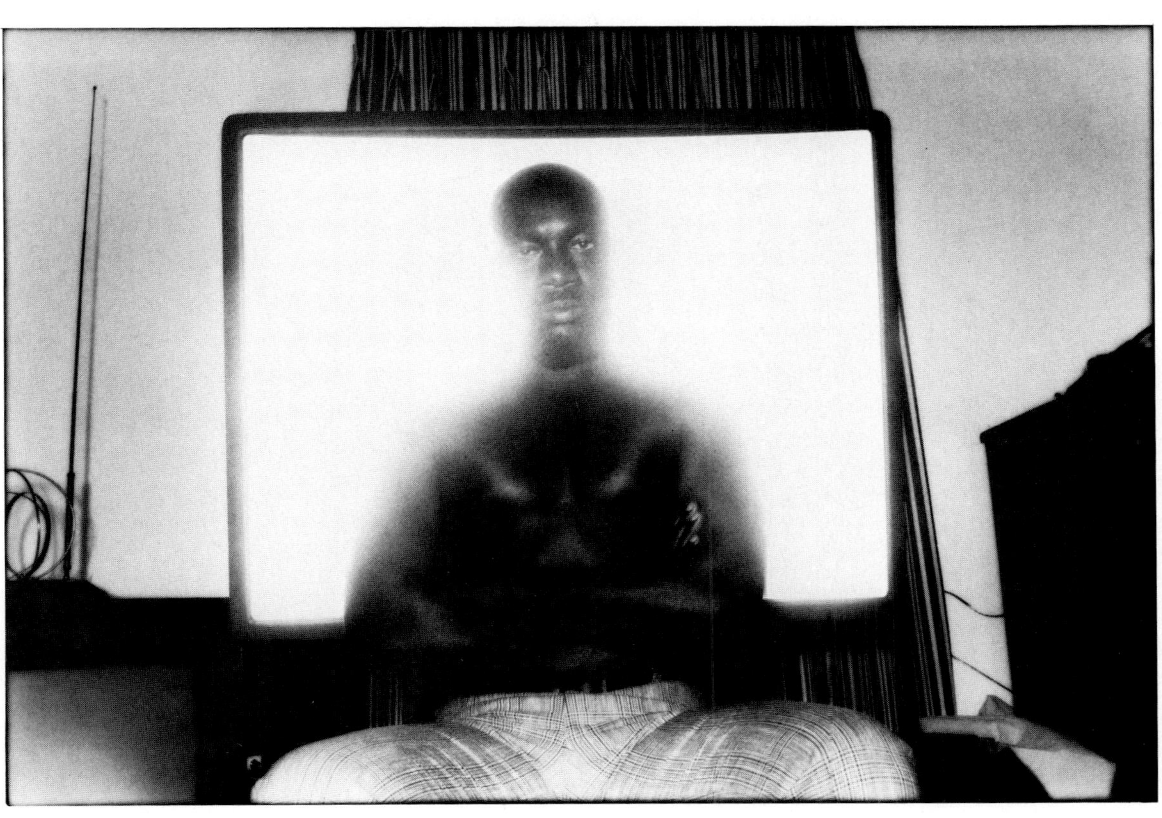

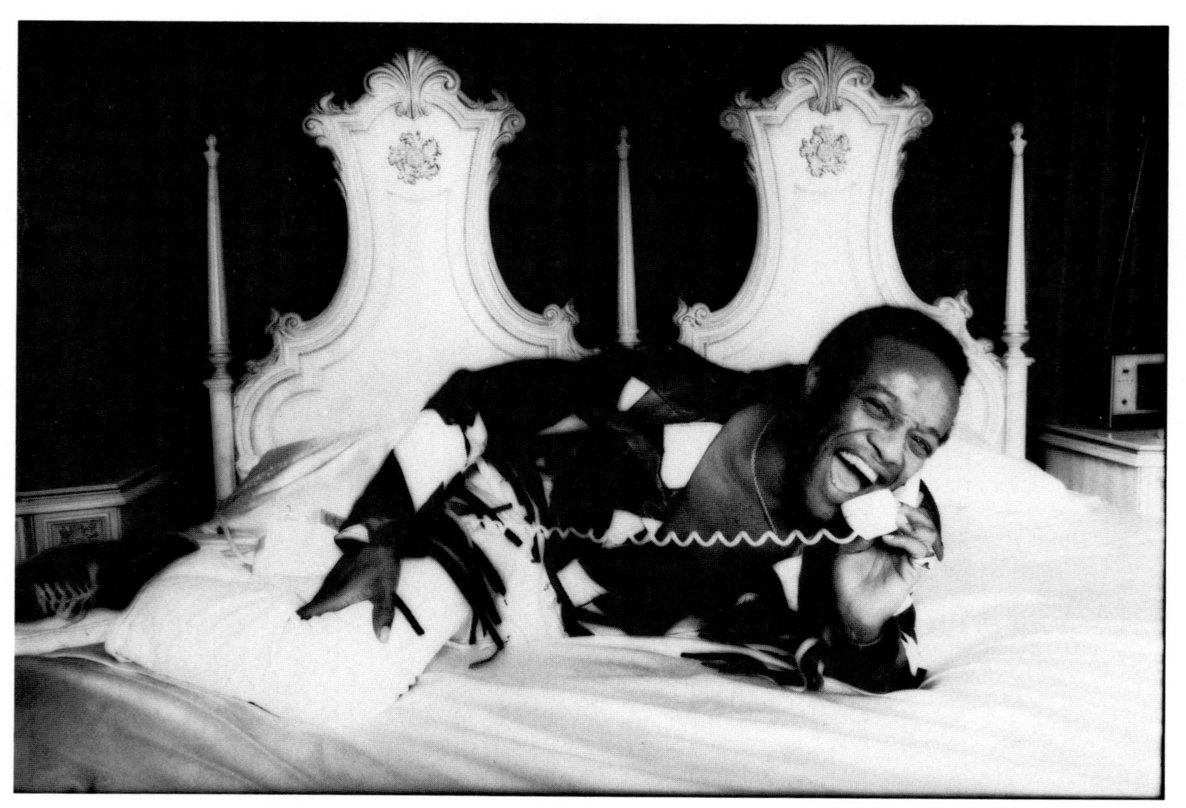

30

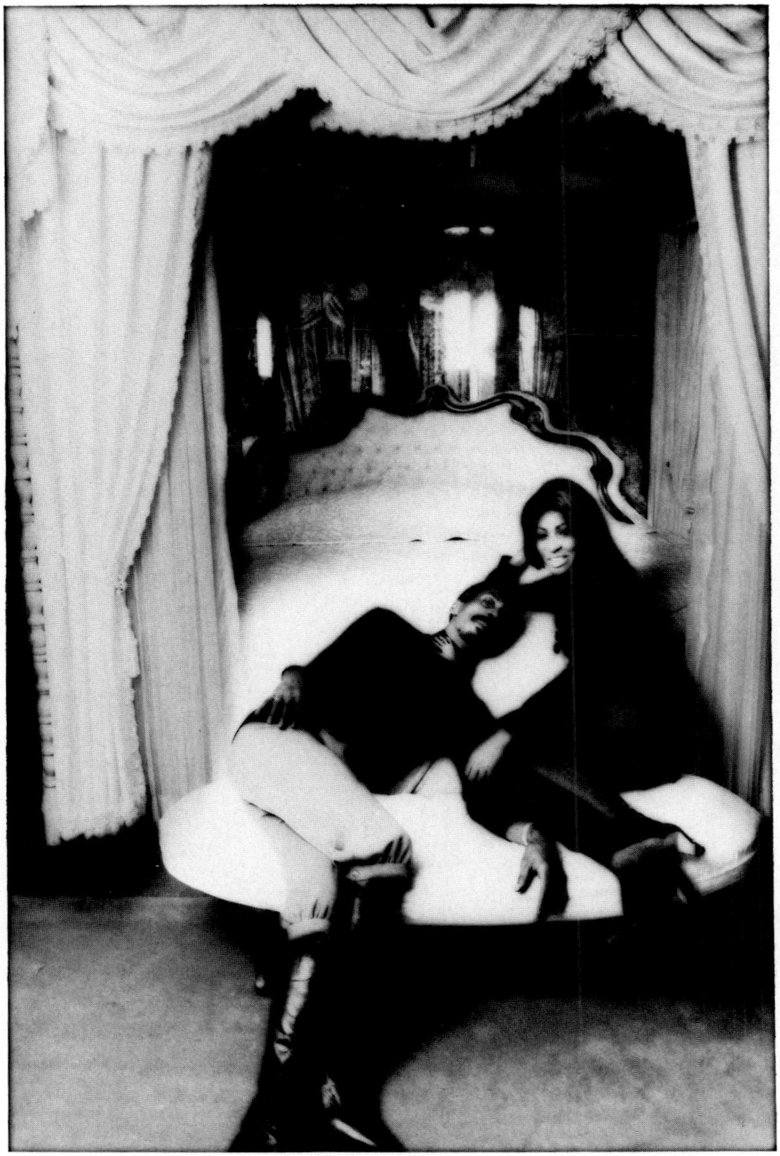

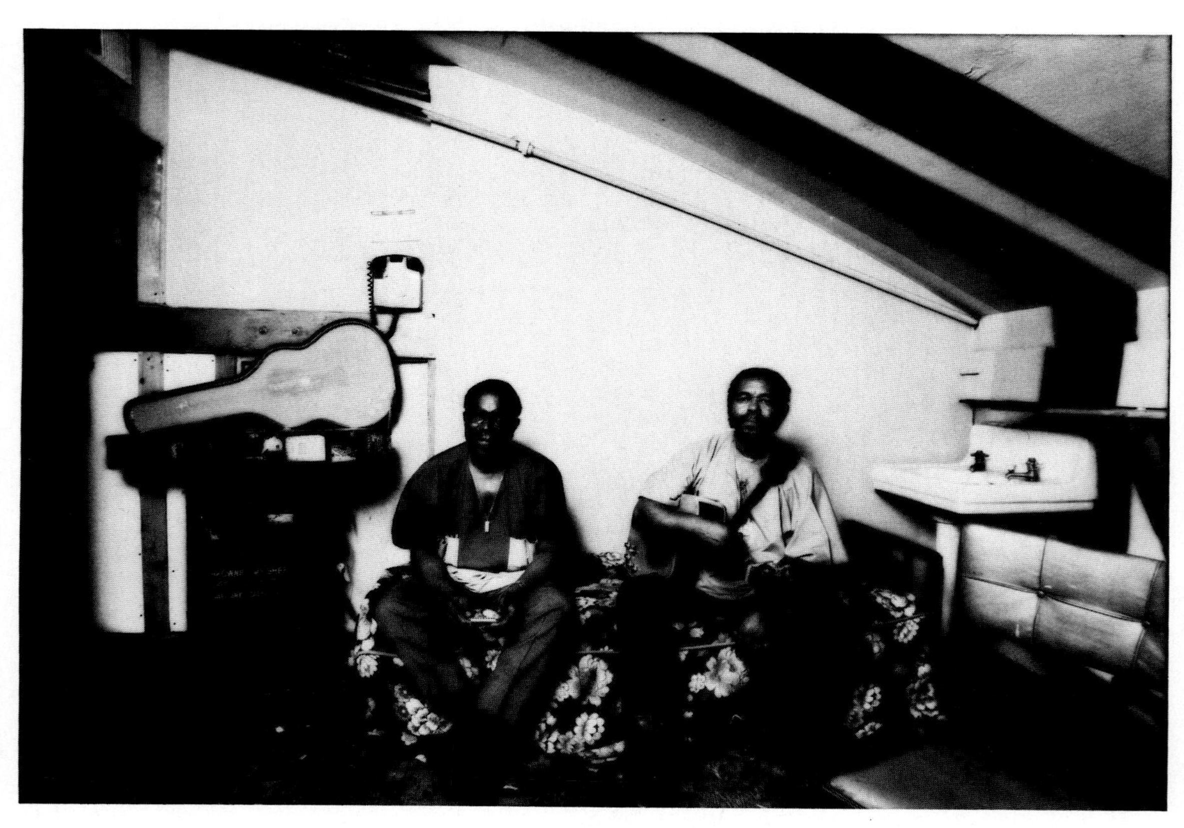

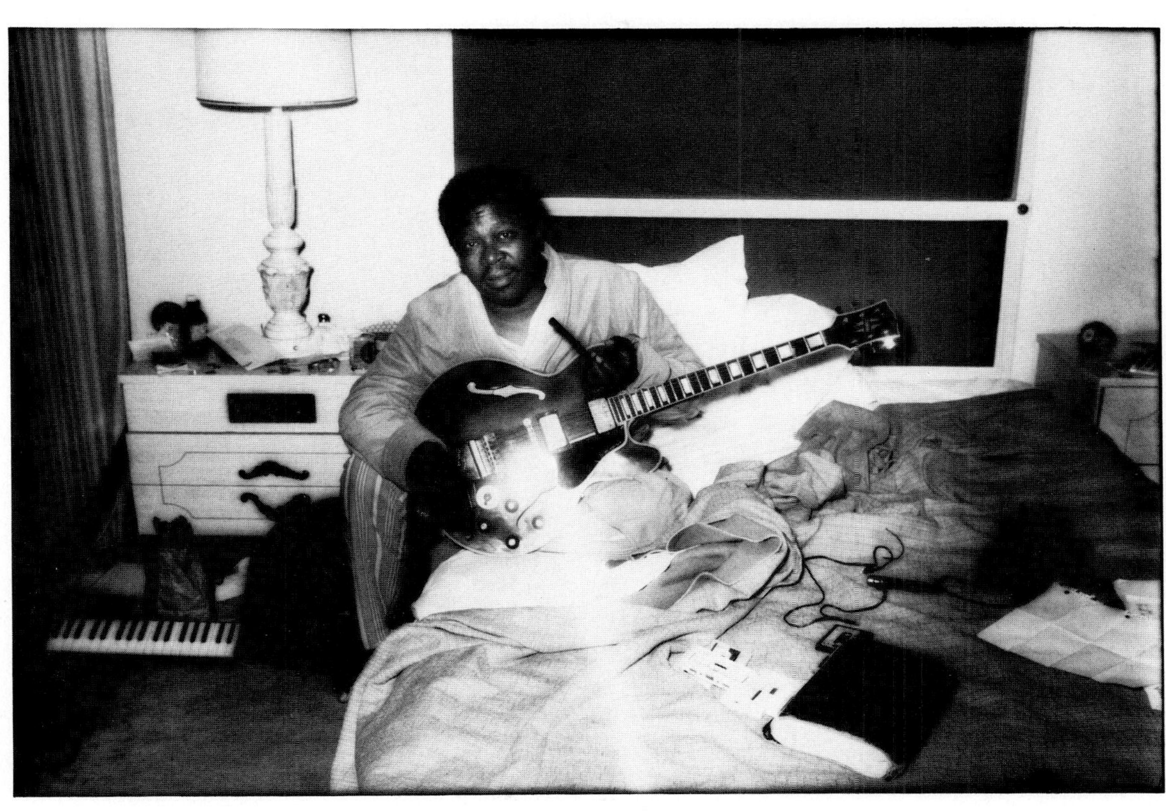

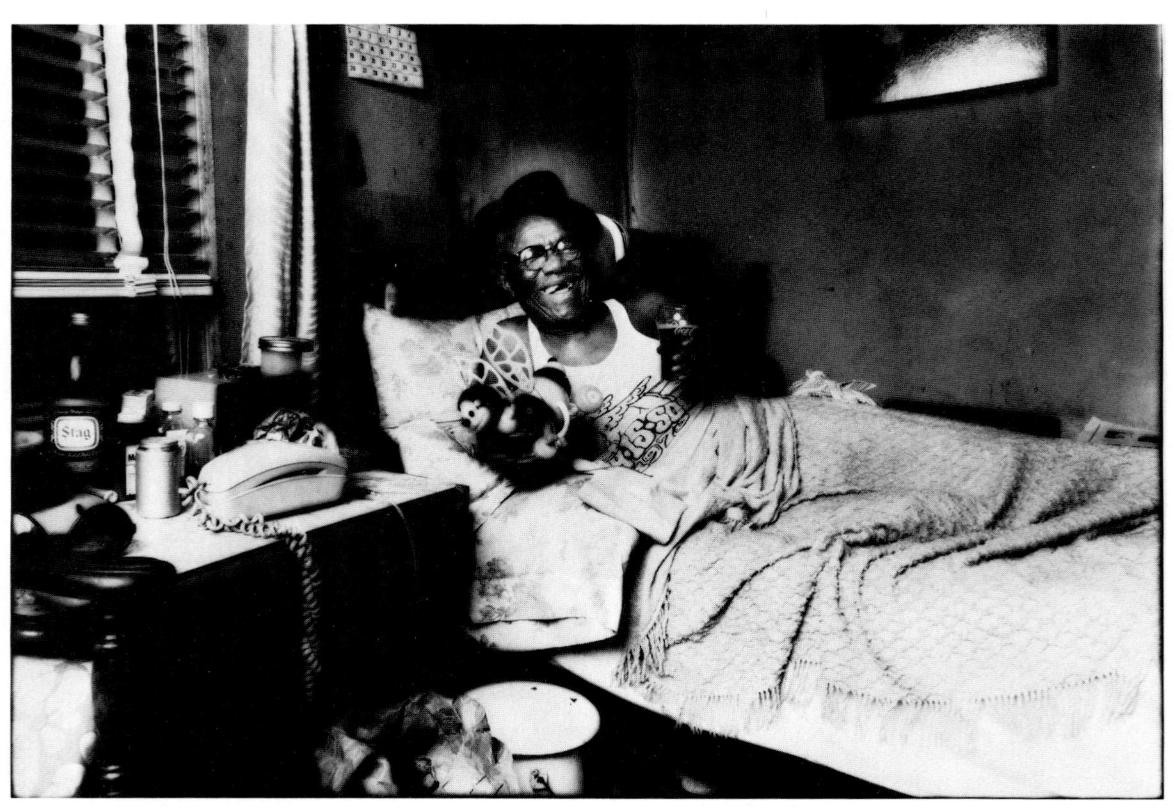
Stag

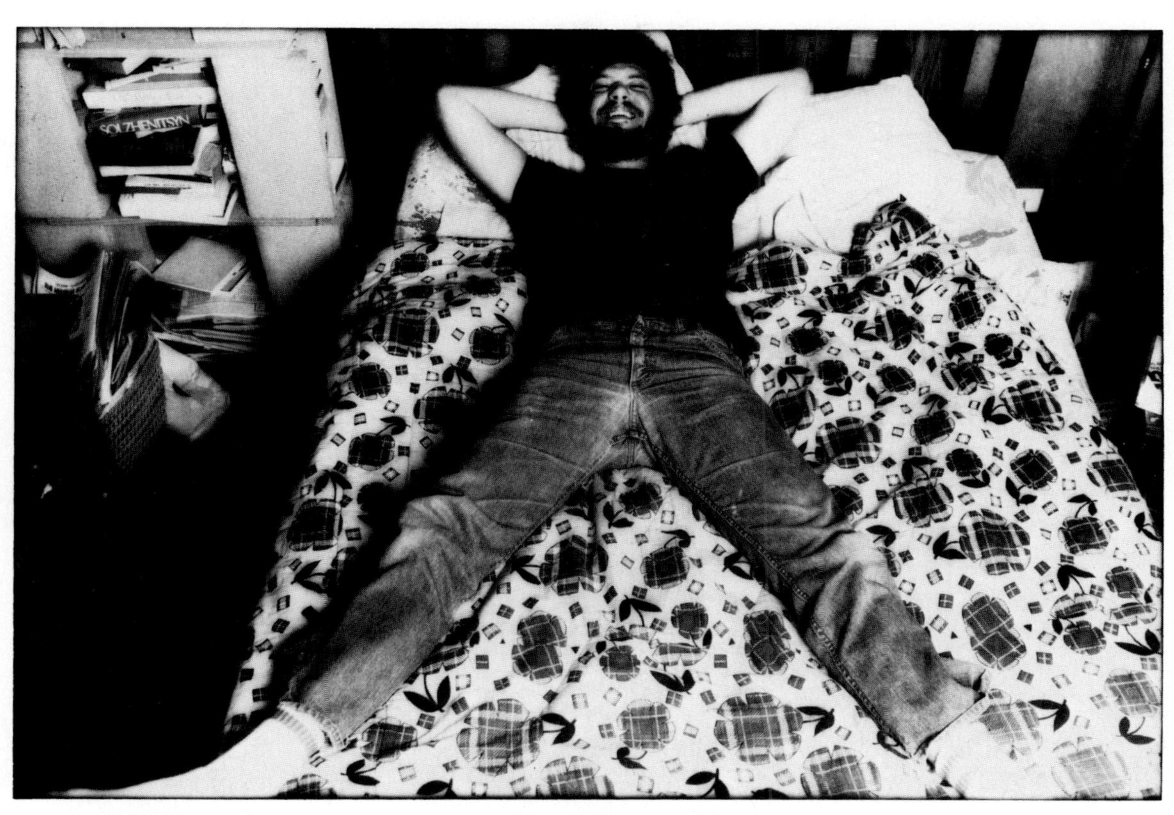
SOLZHENITSYN

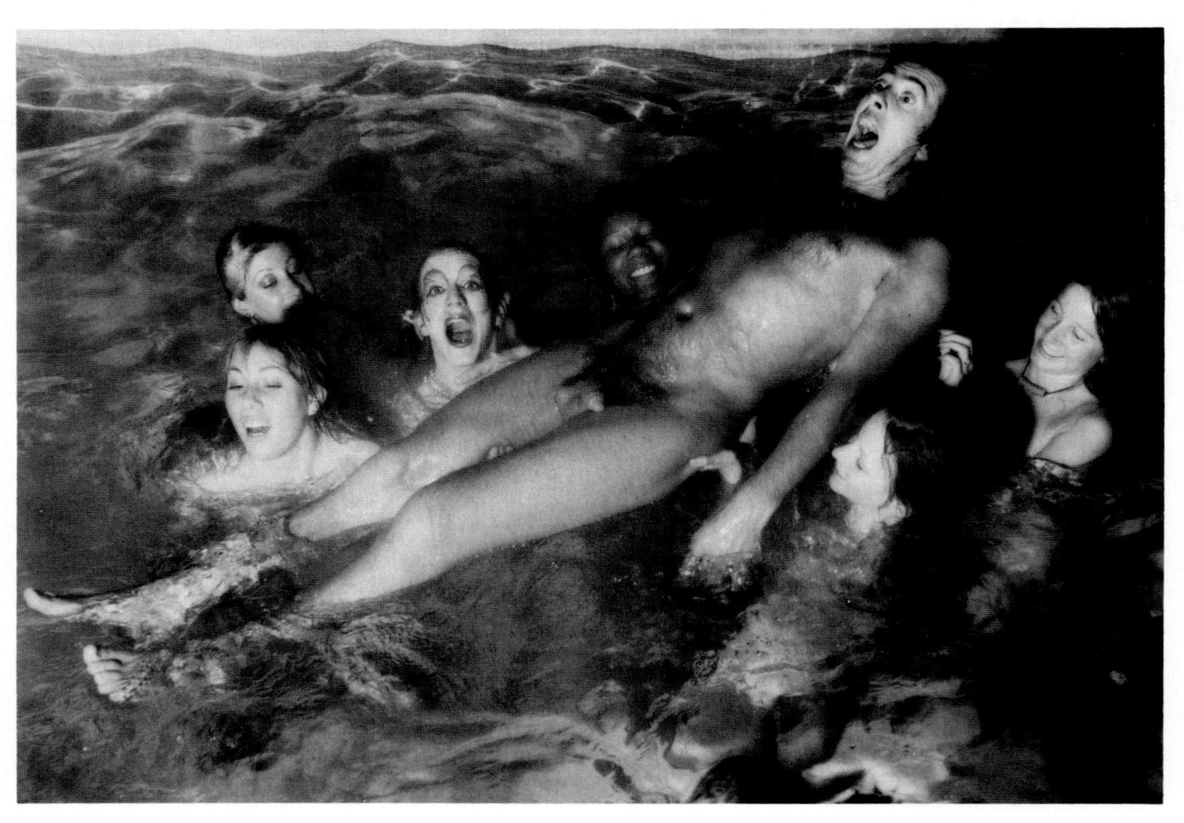

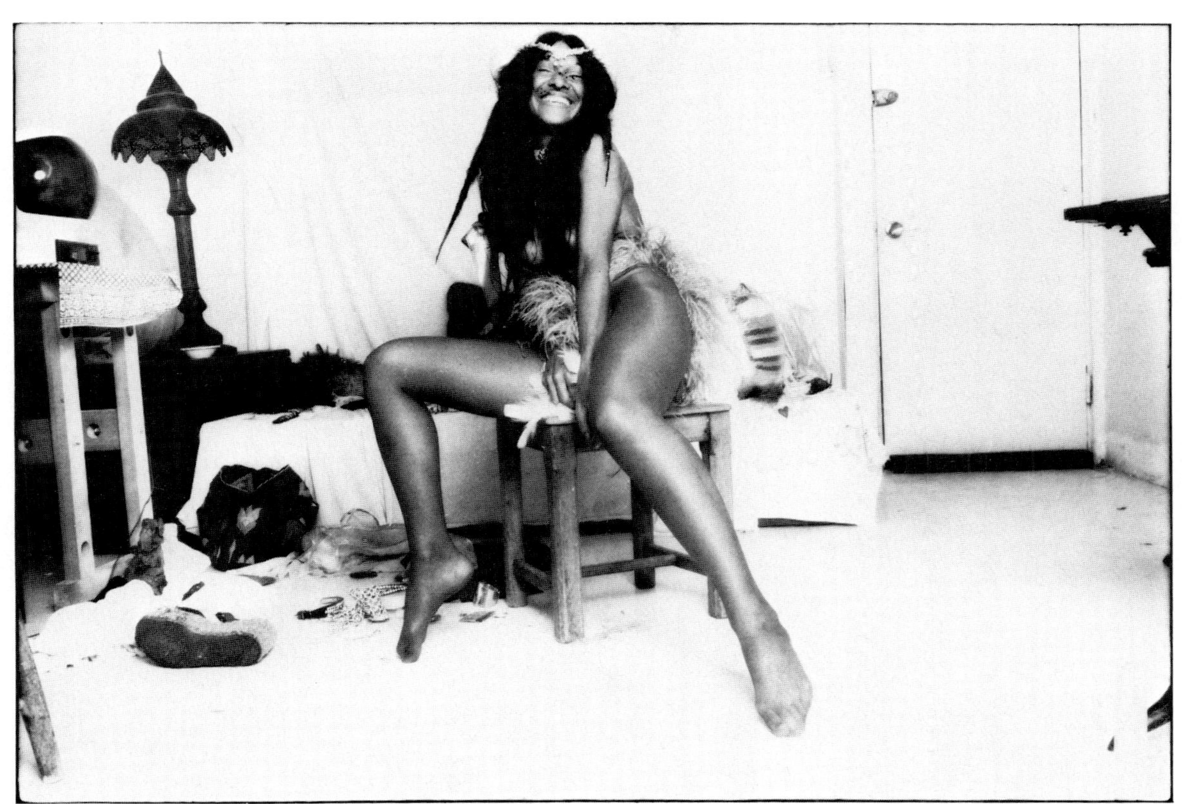

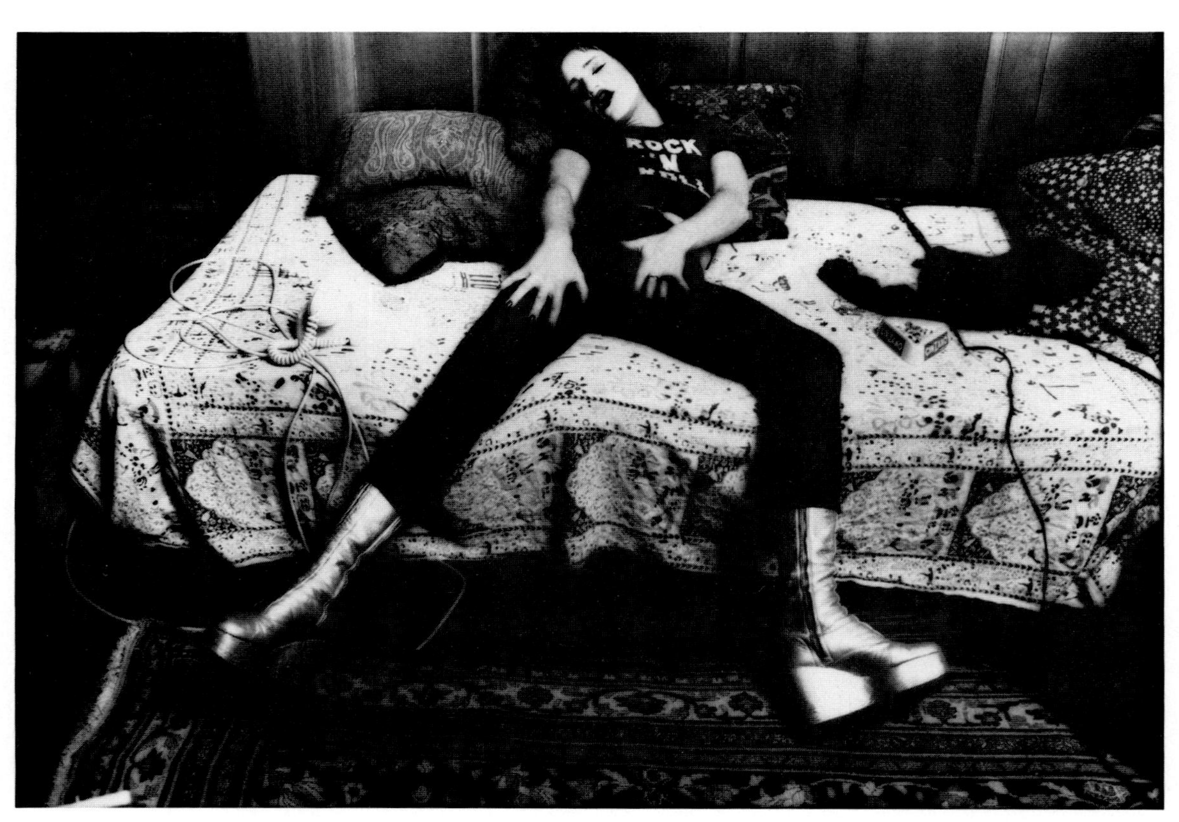
ROCK

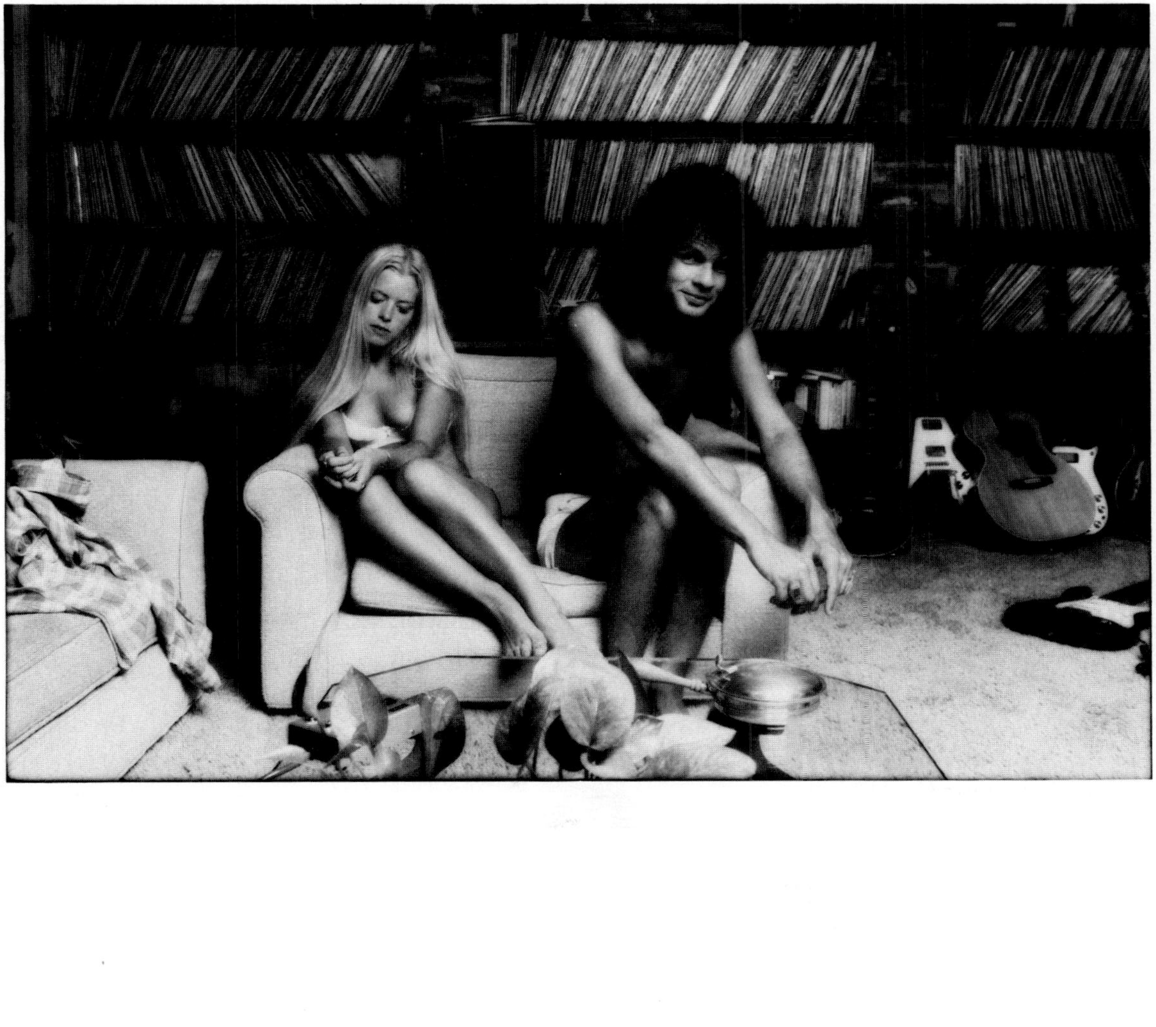

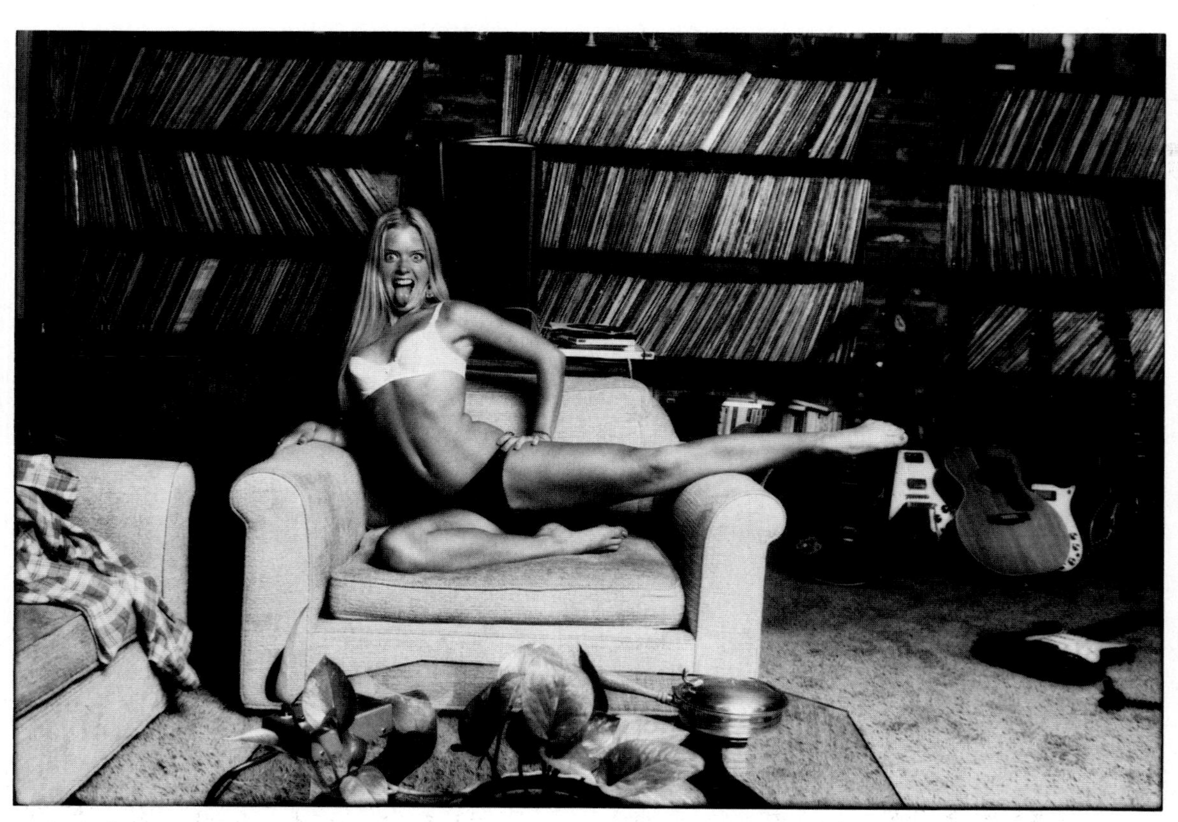

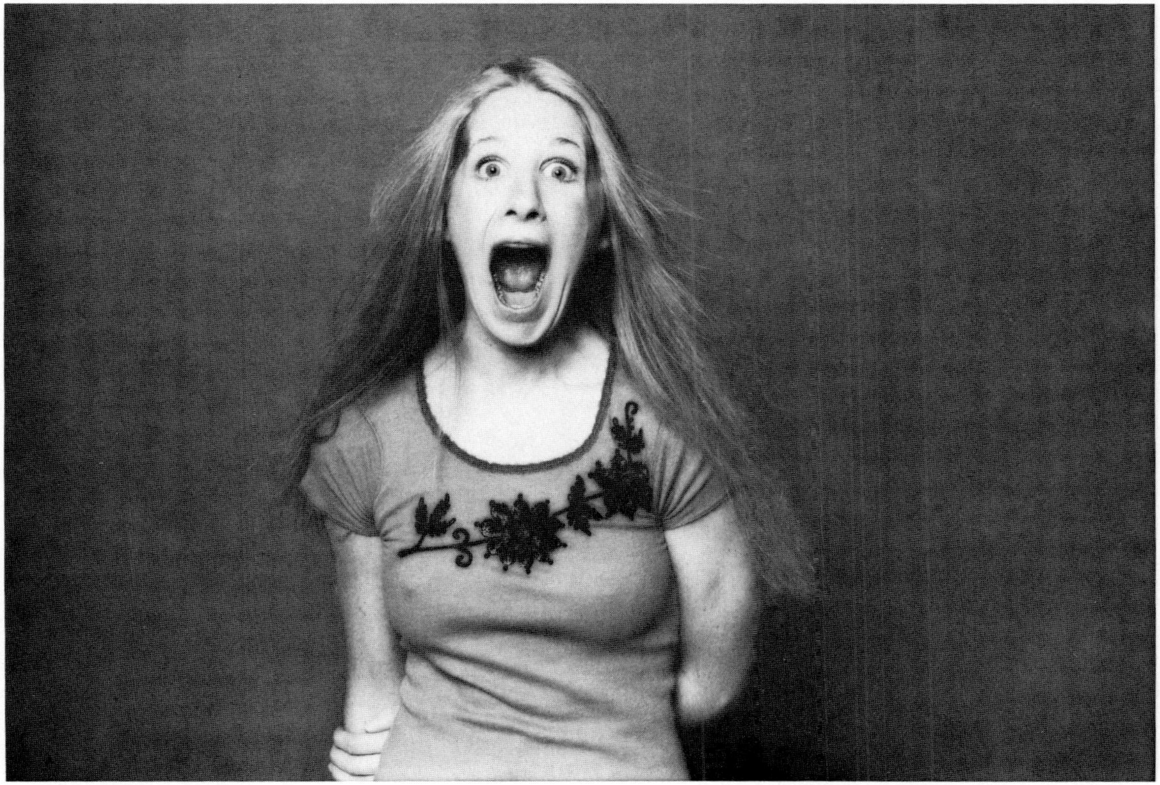

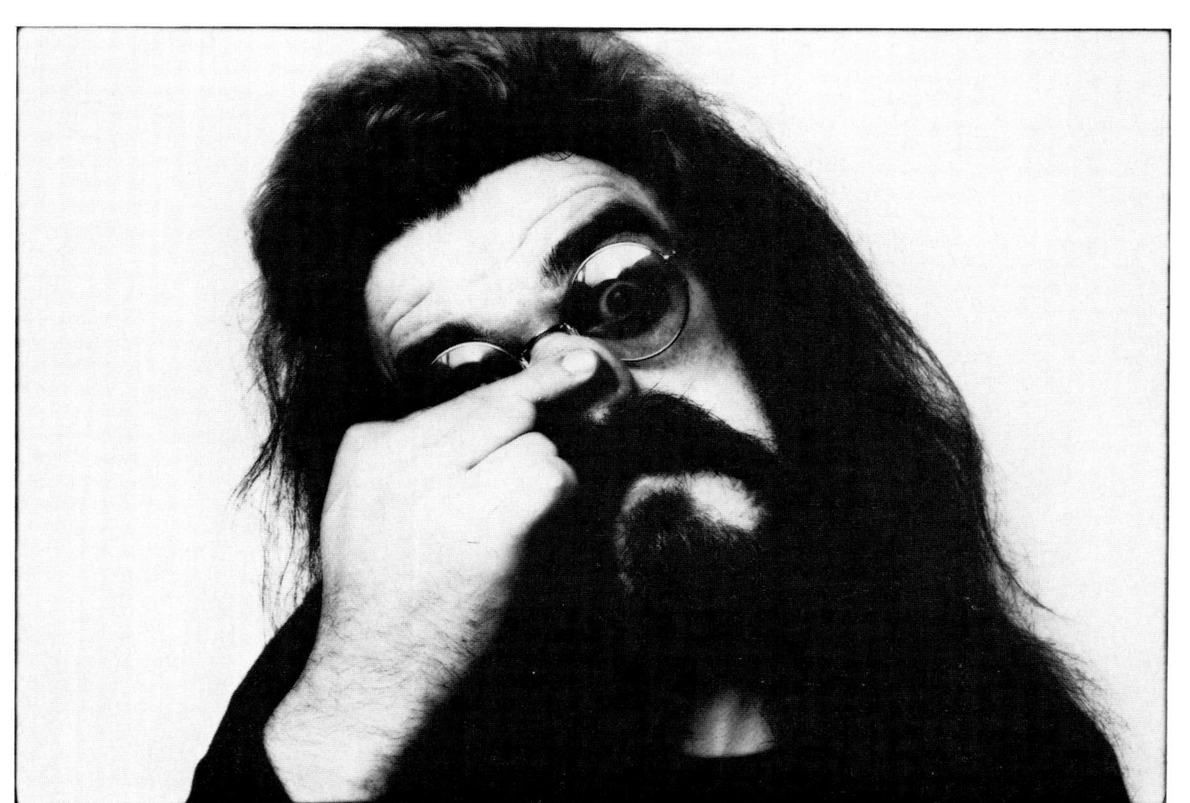

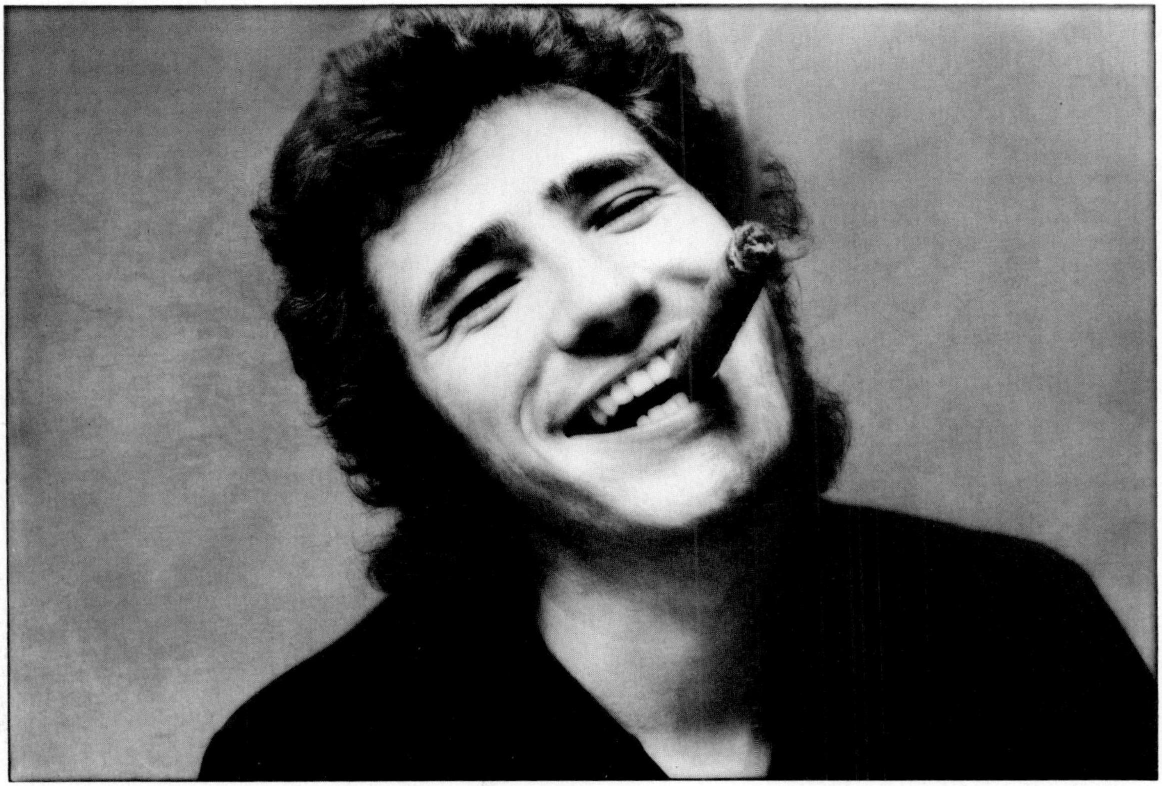

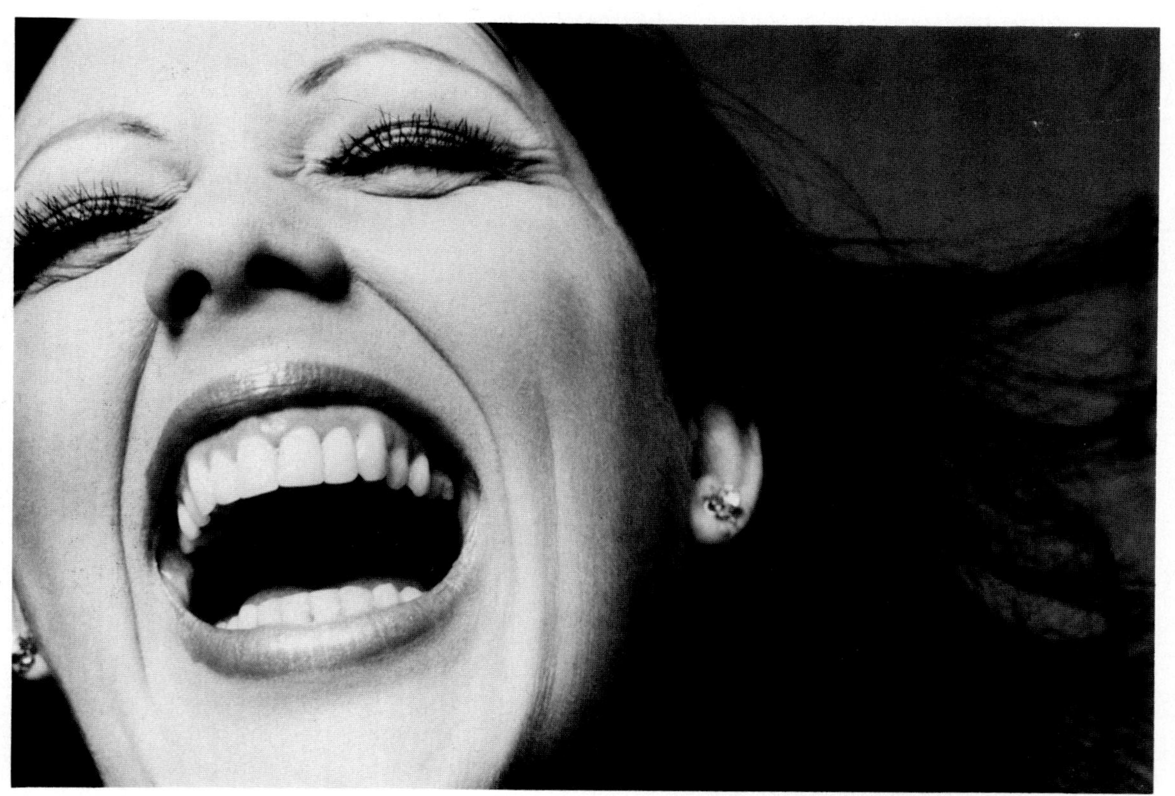

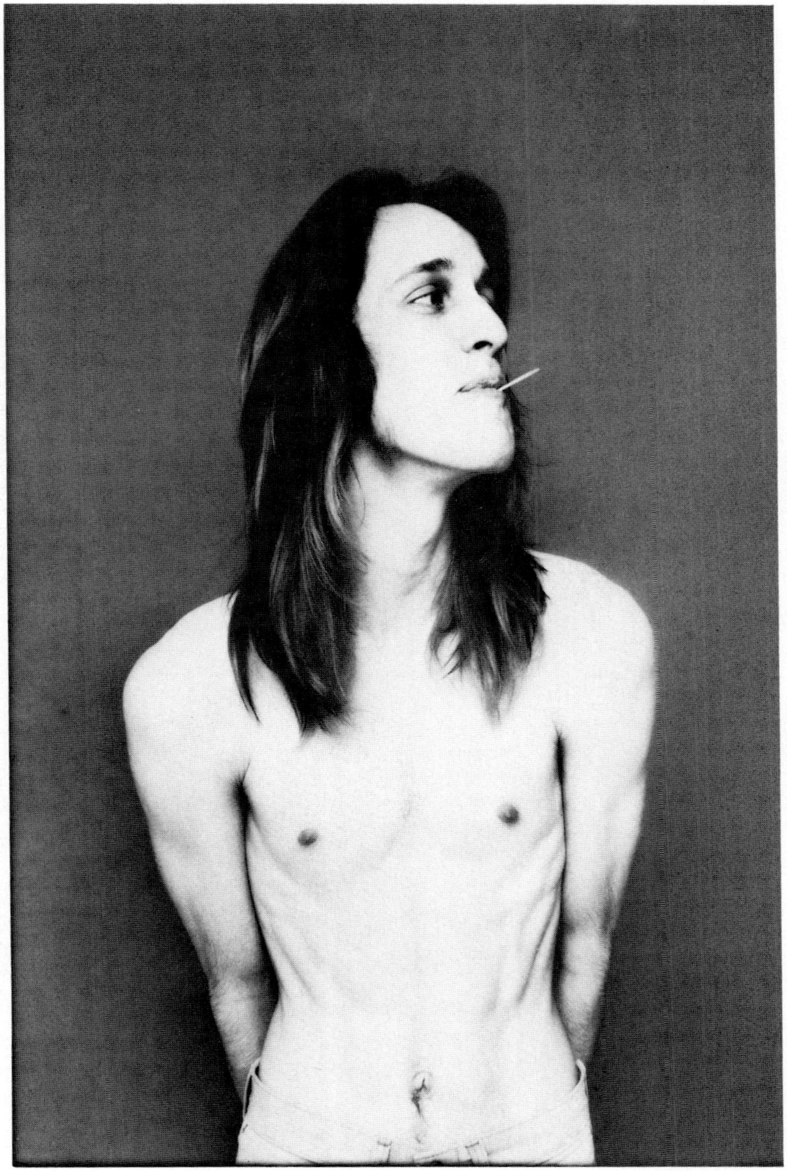

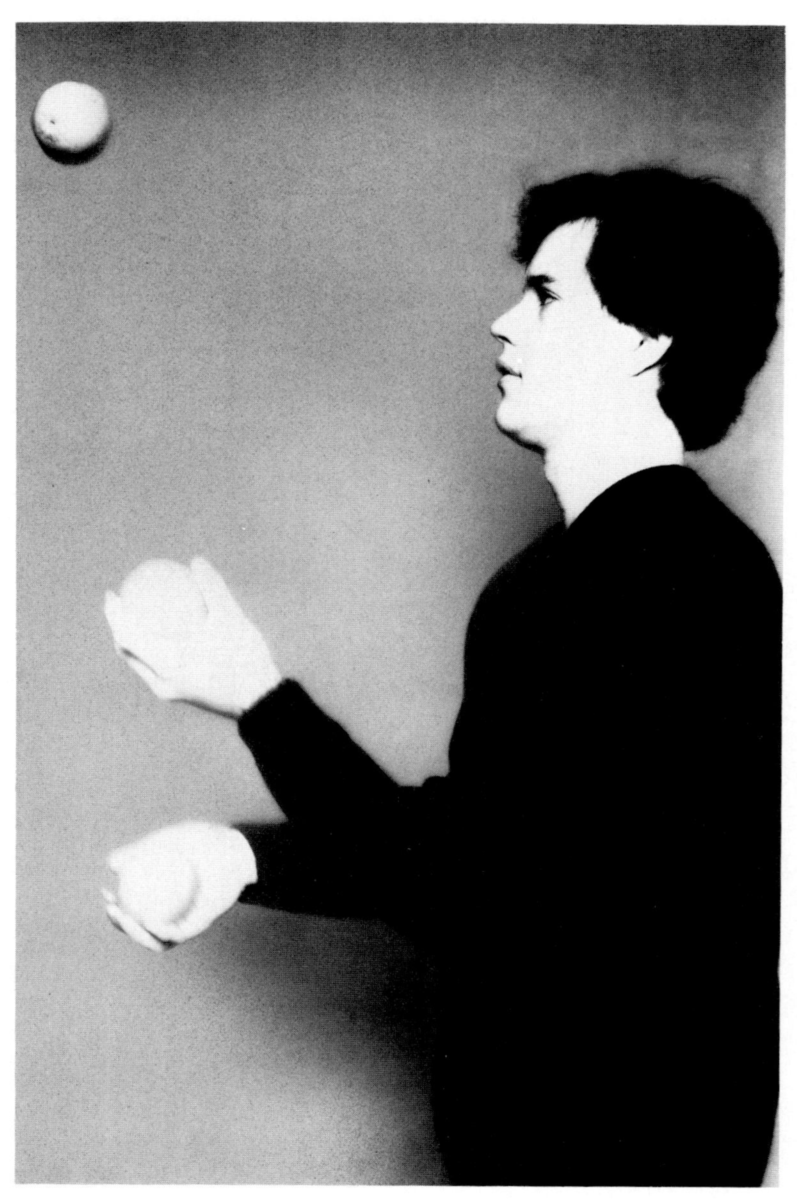

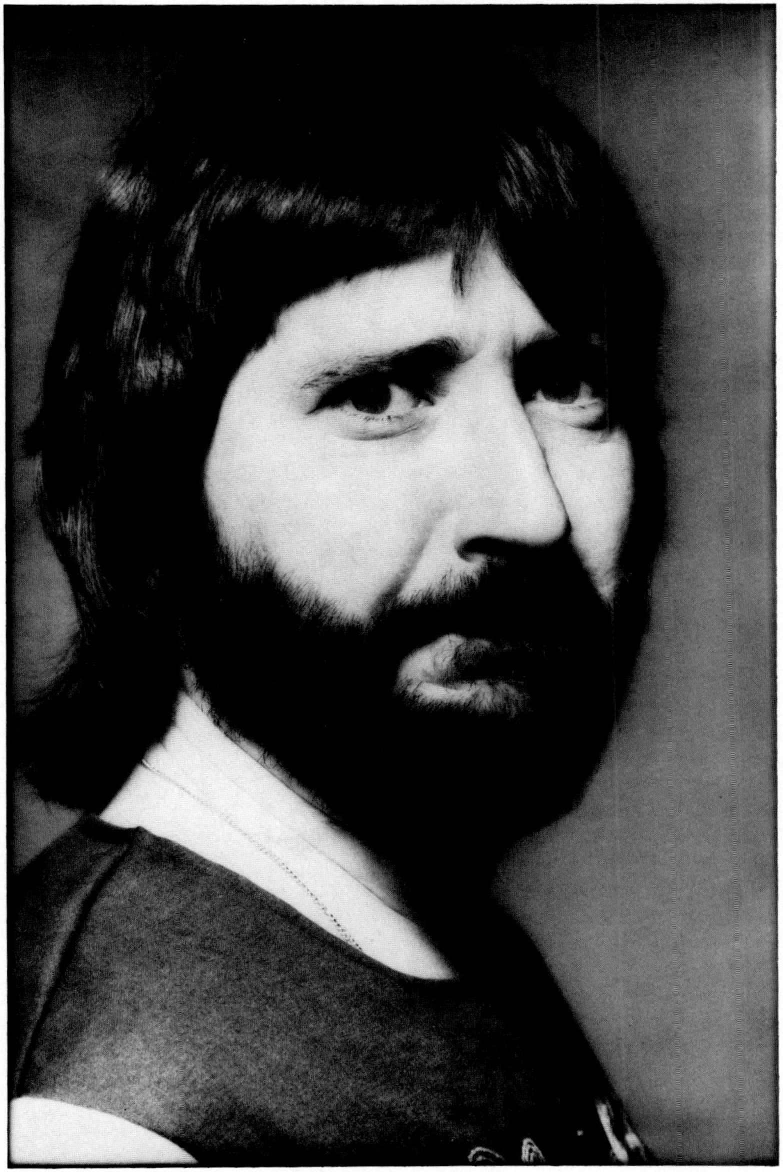

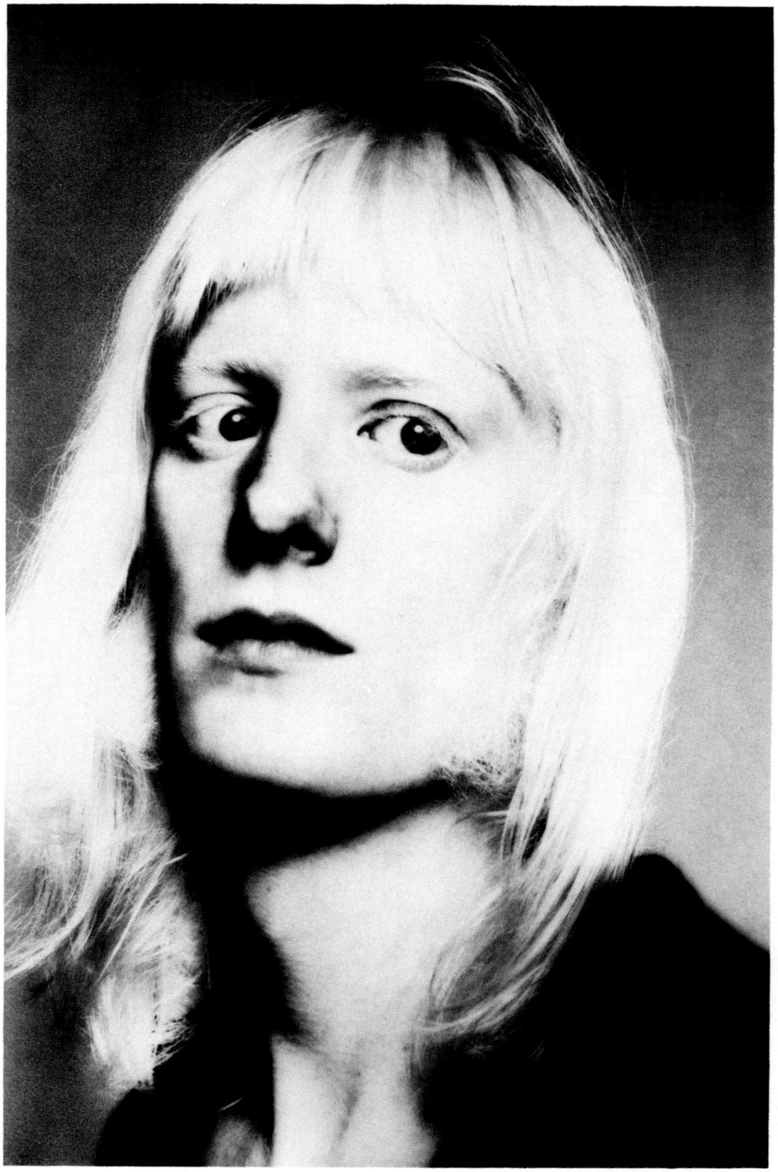

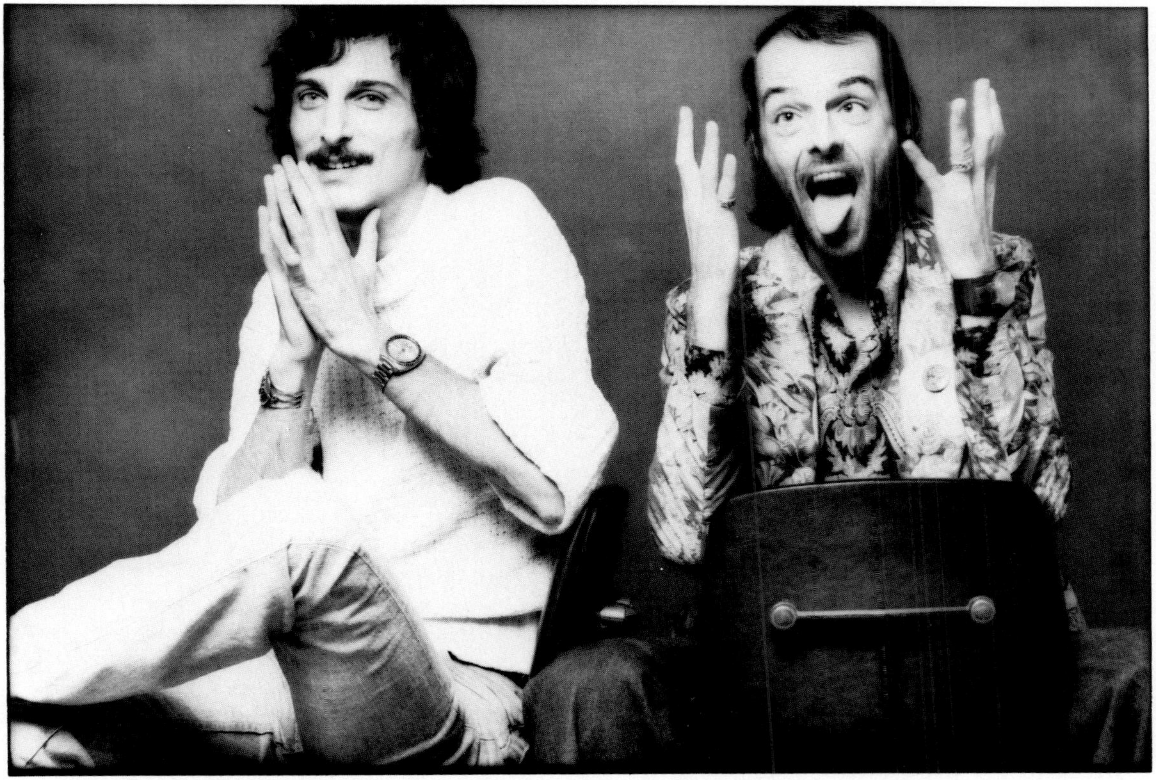

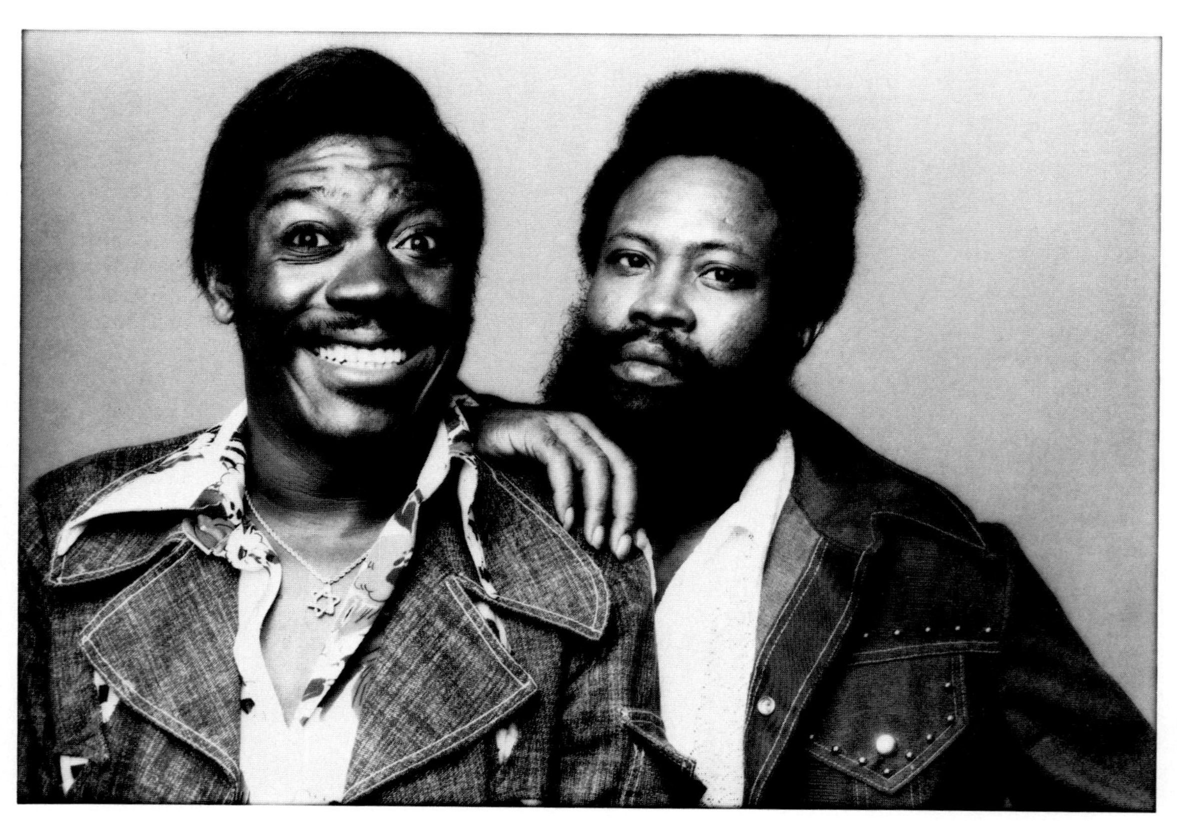

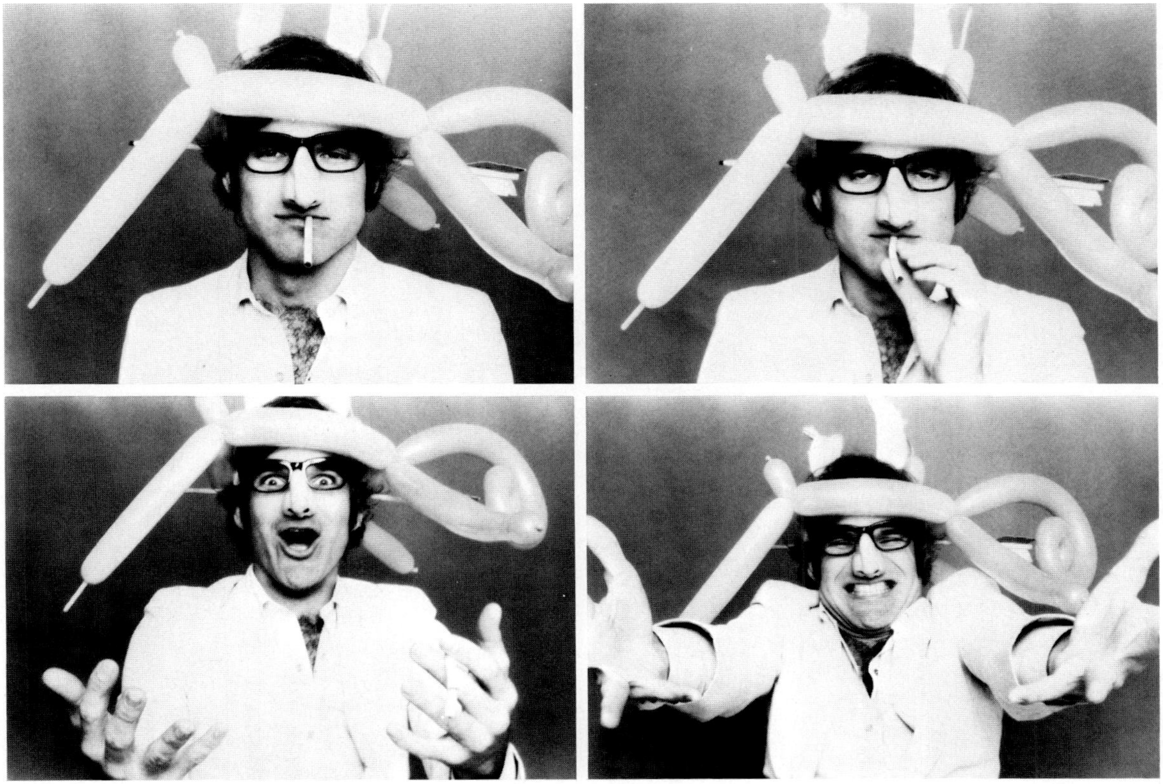

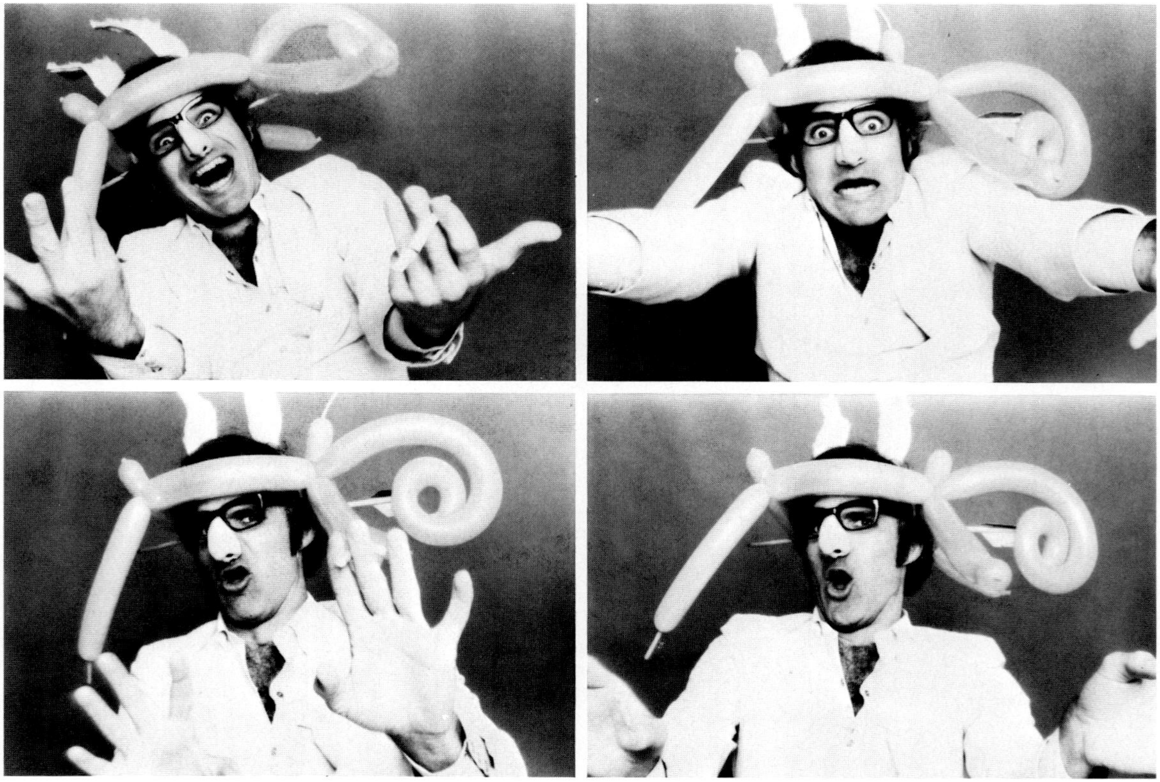

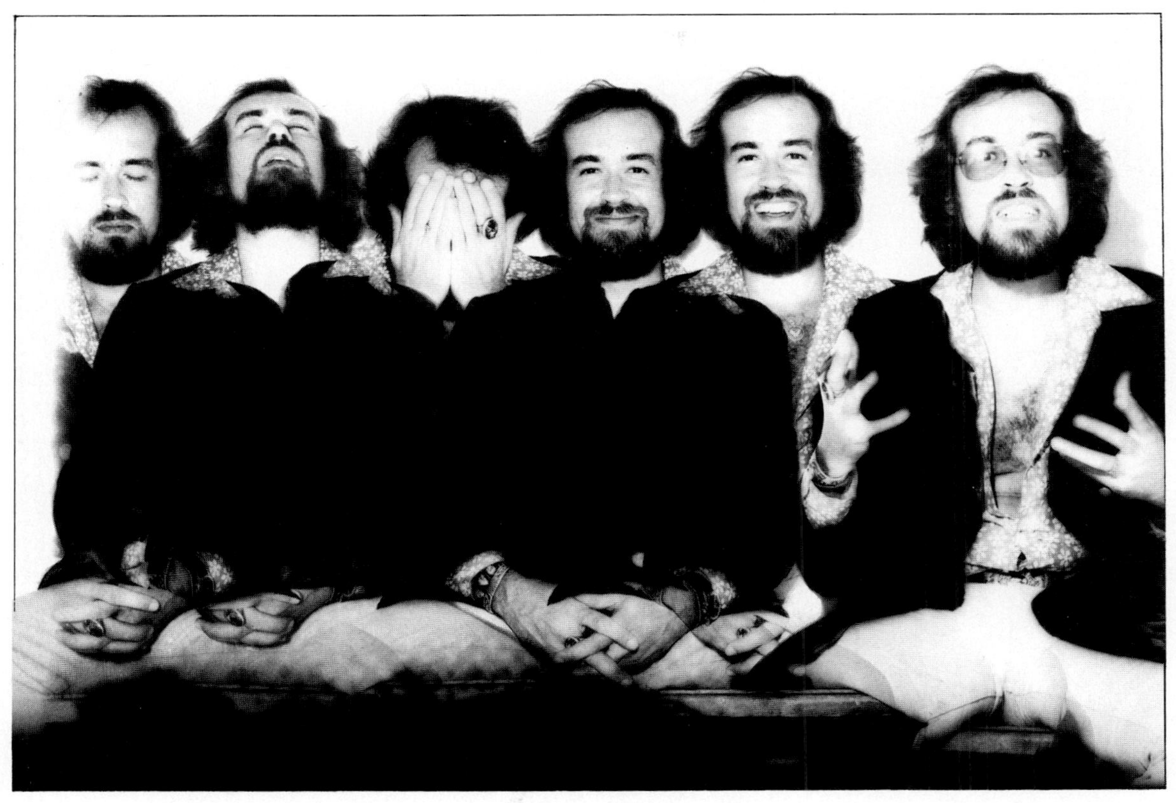

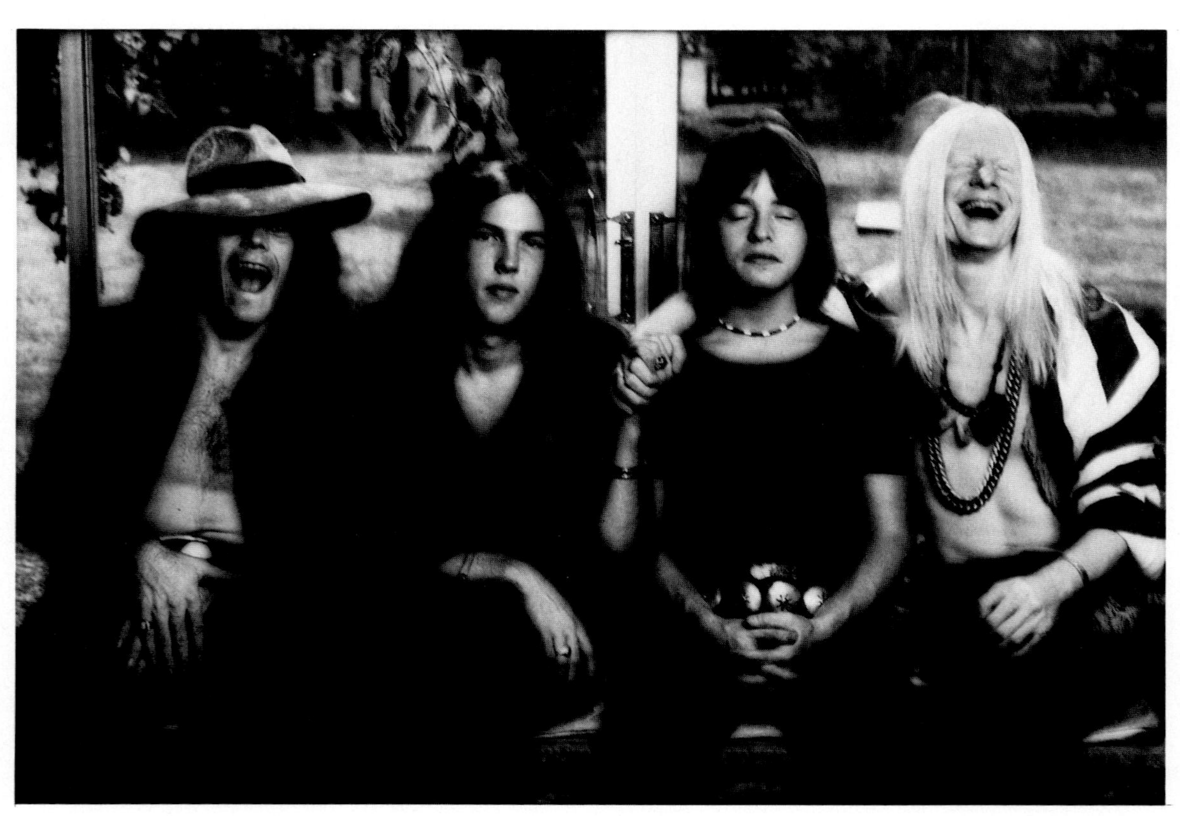

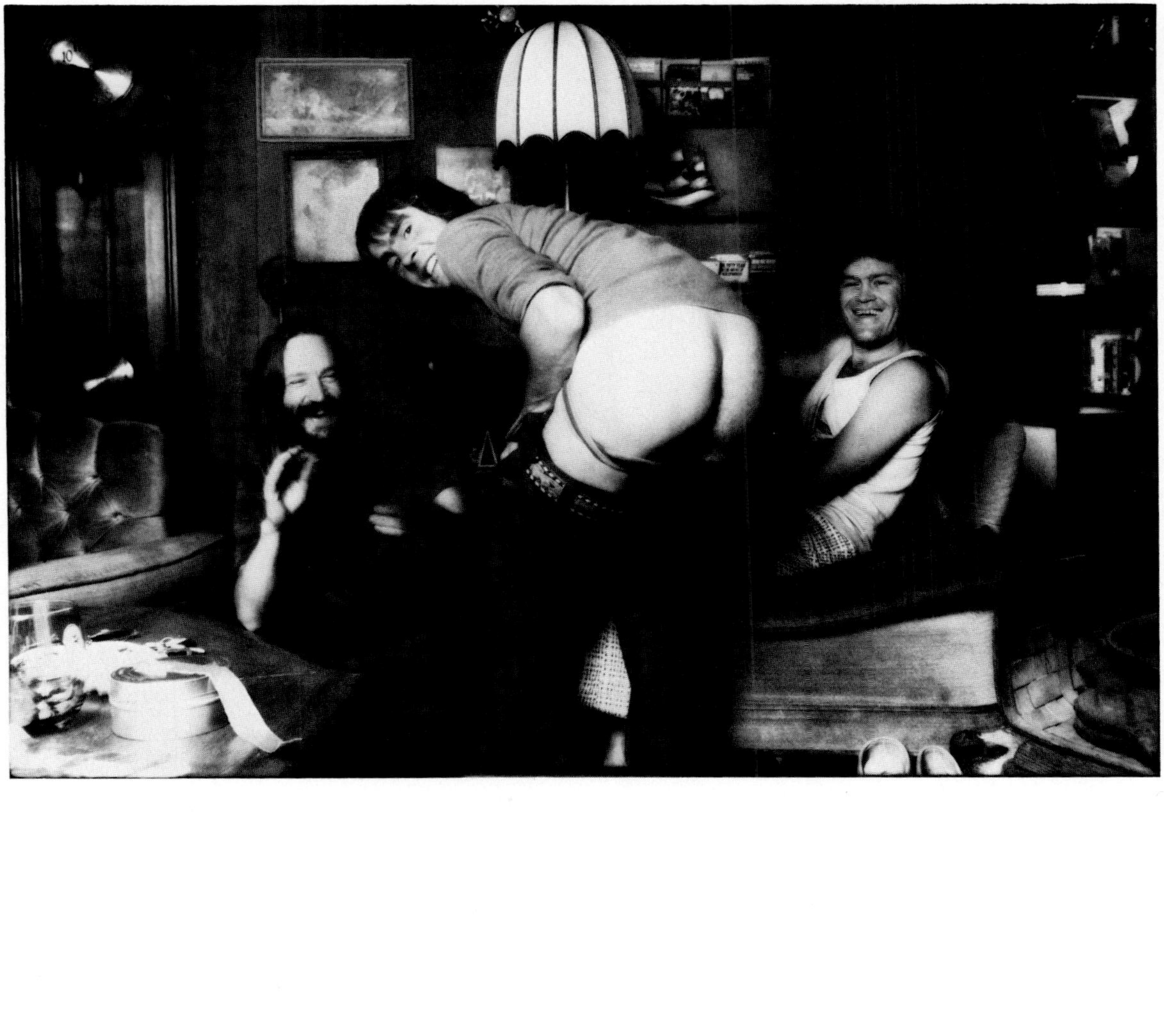

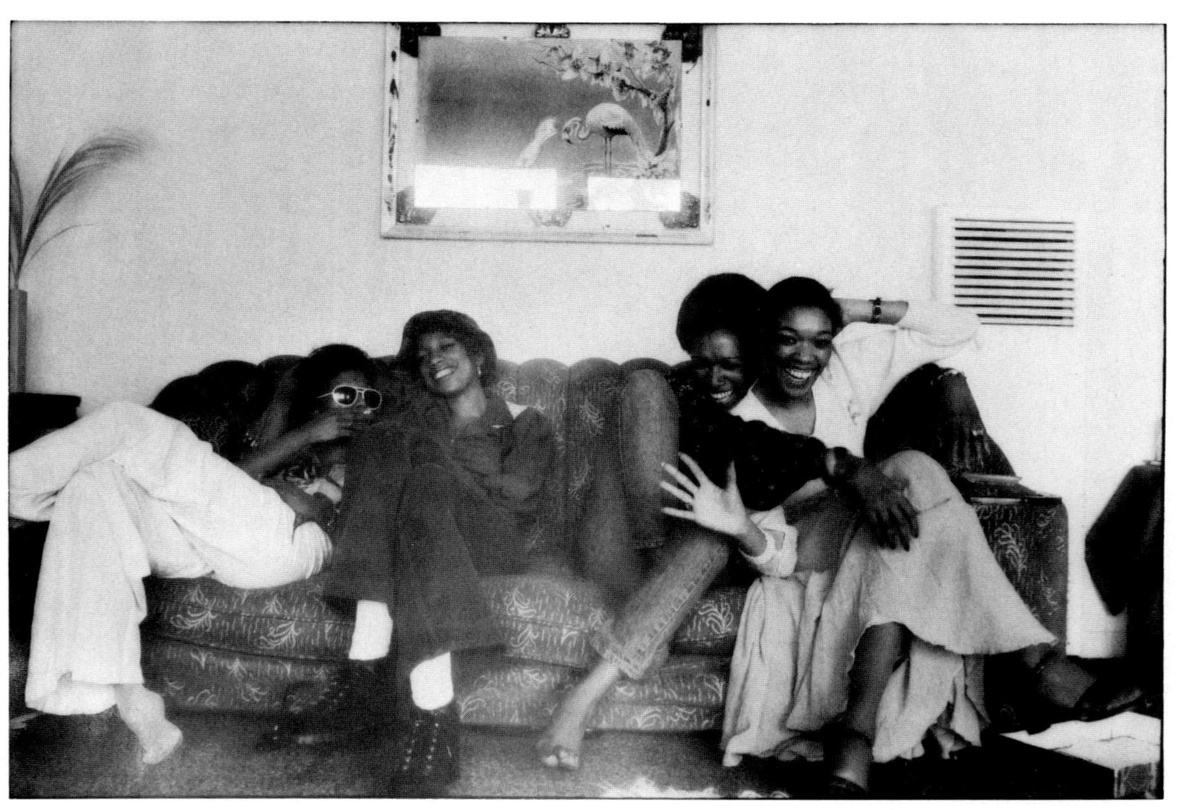

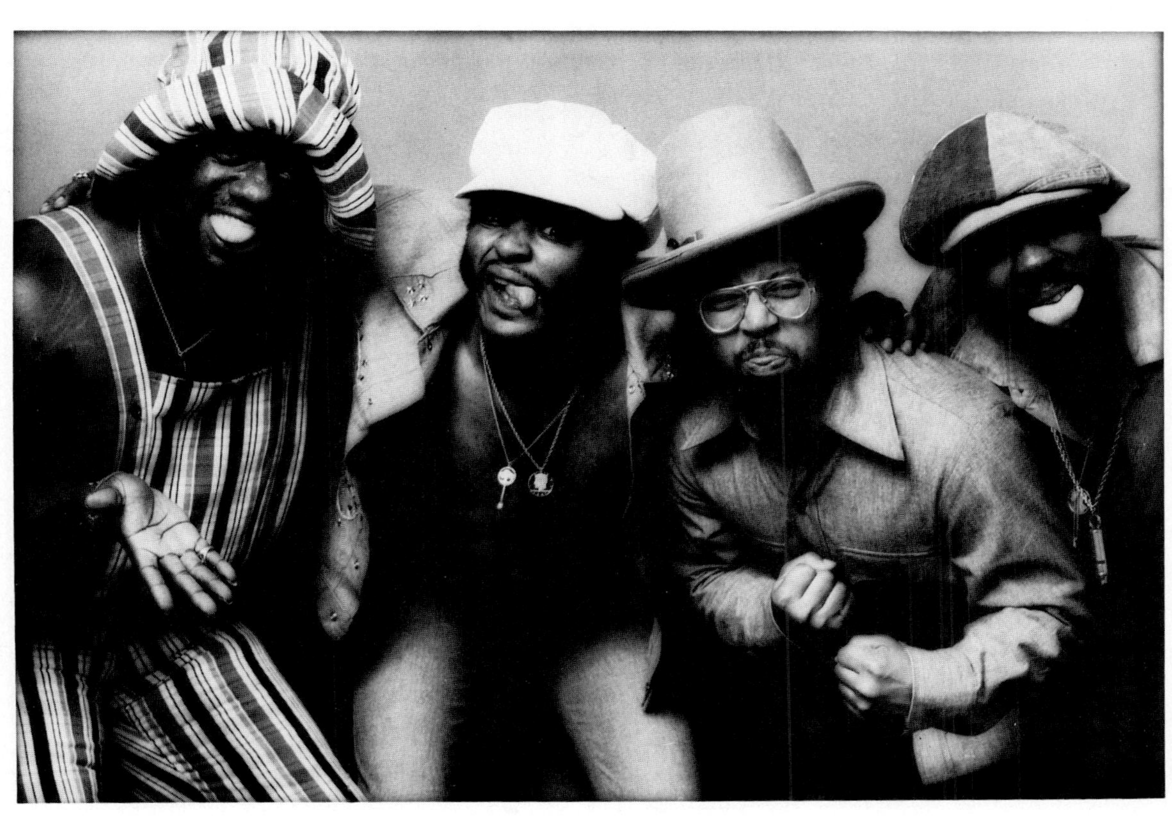

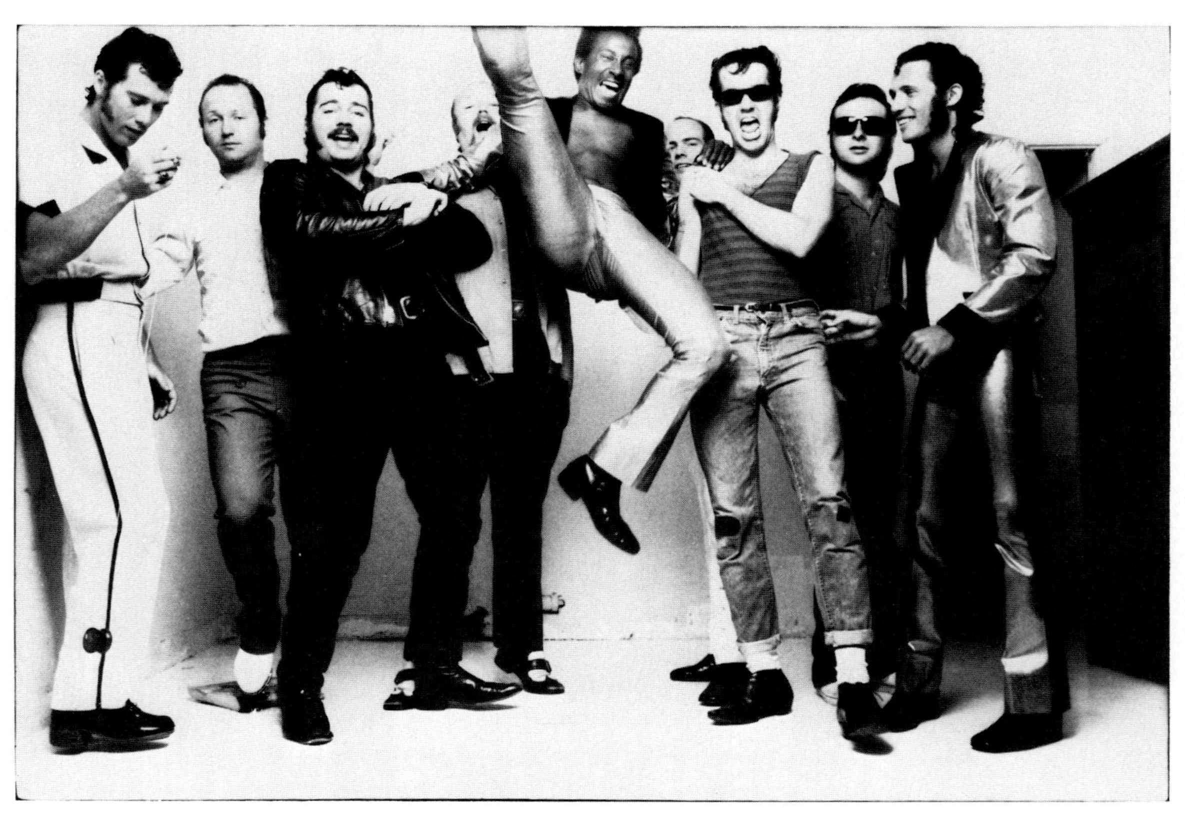

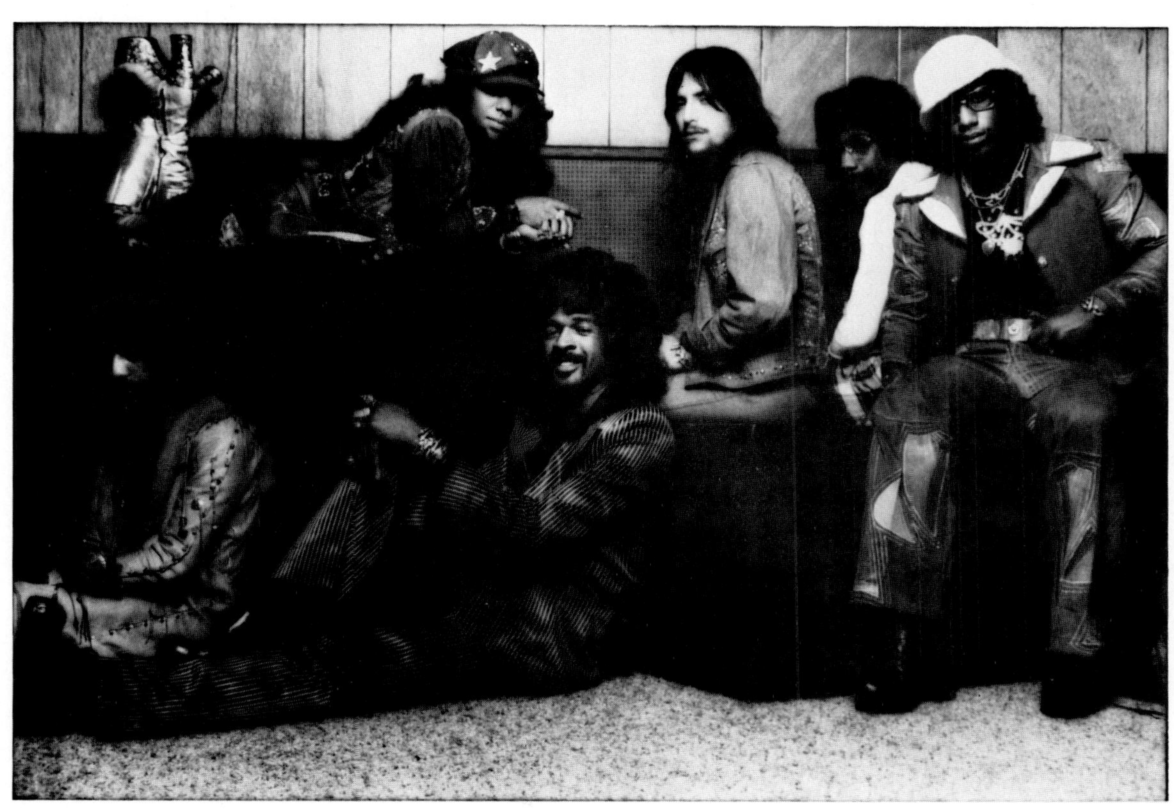

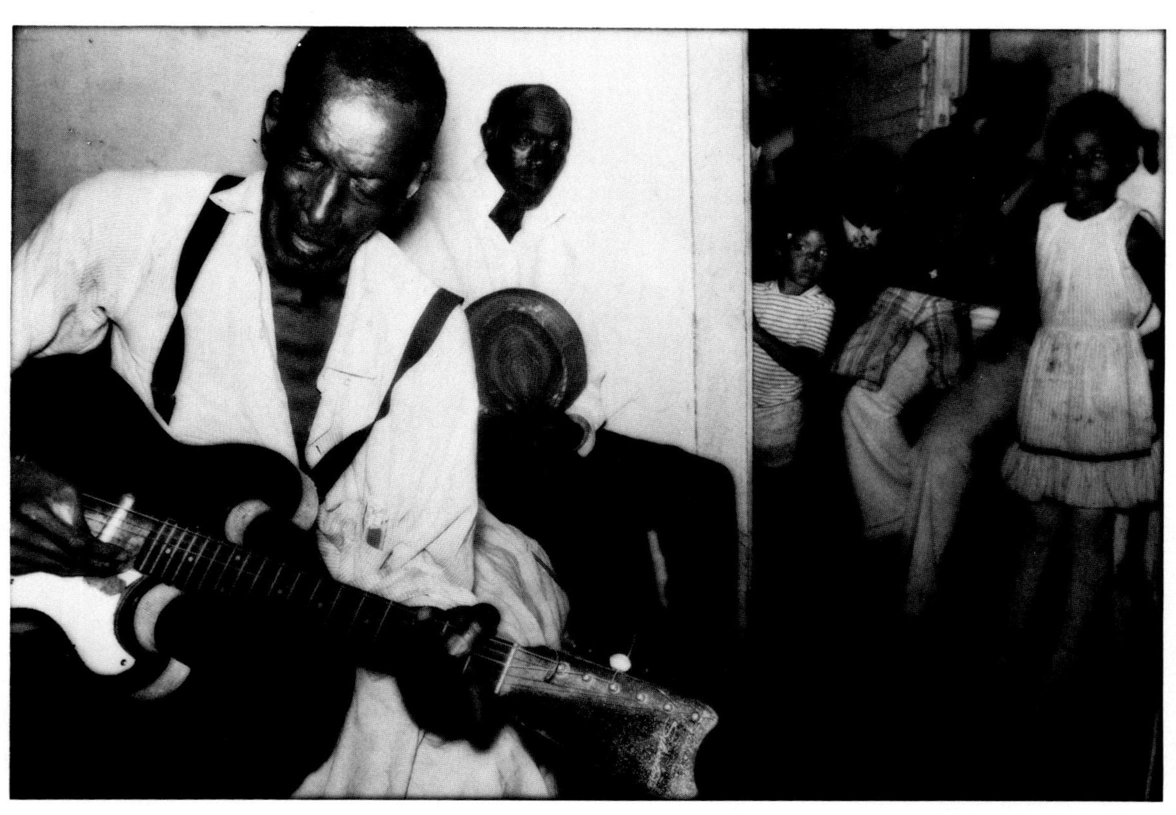

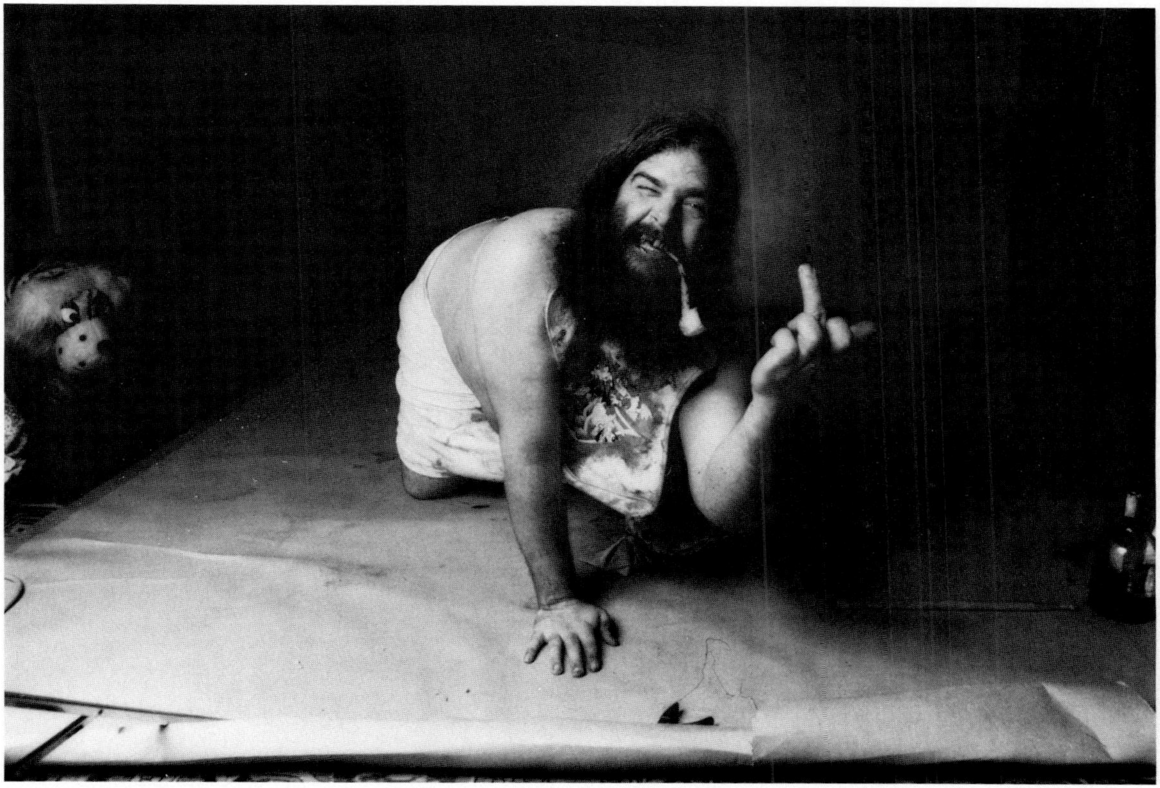

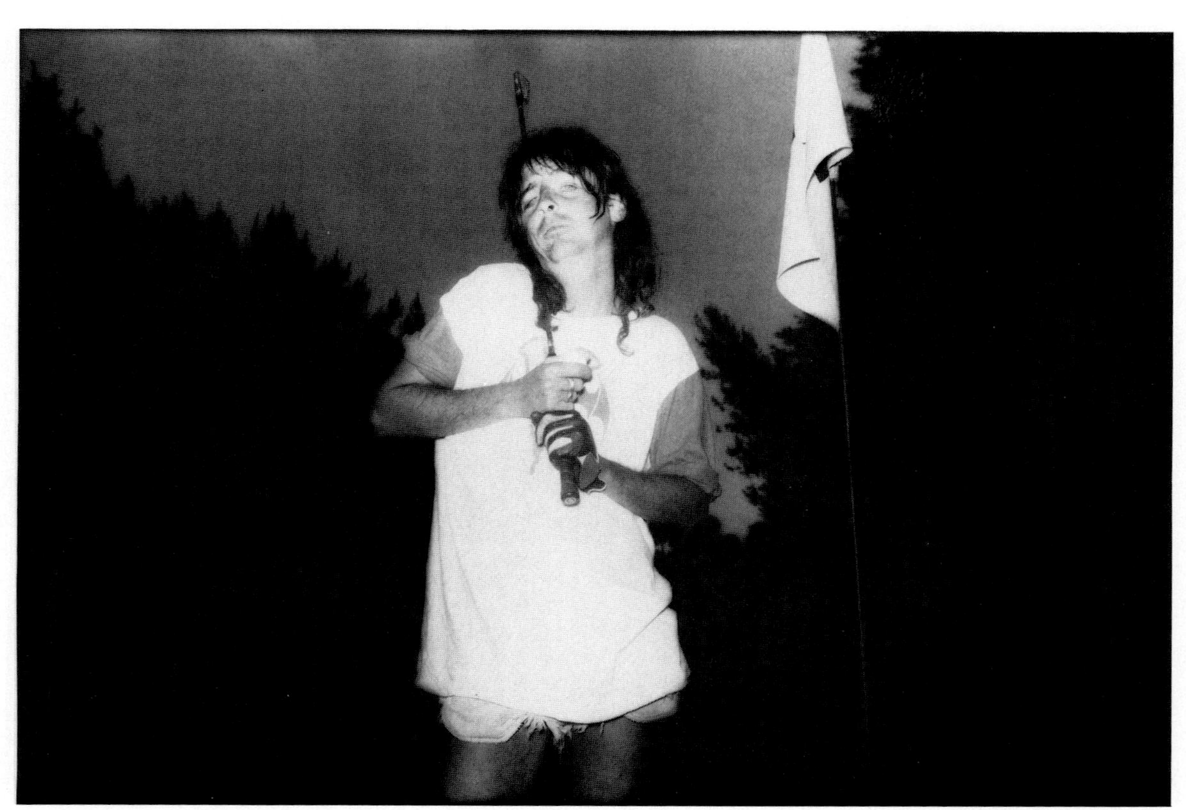

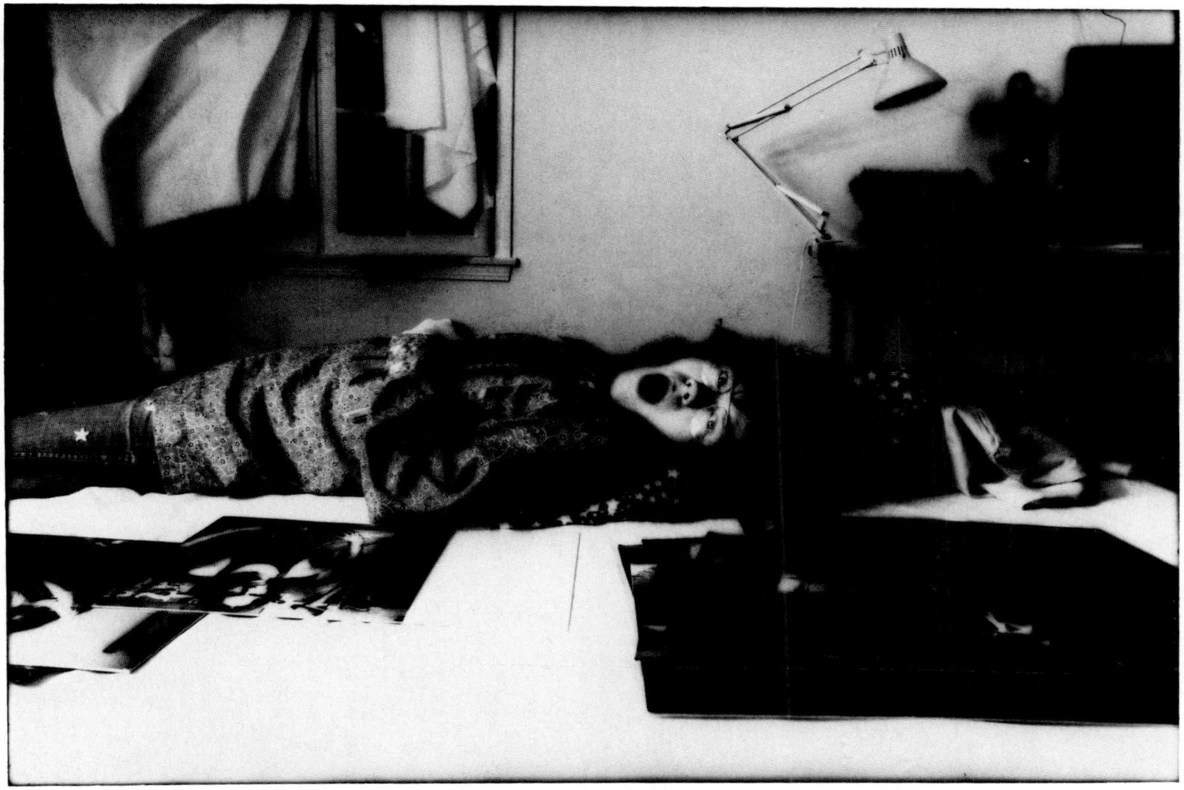

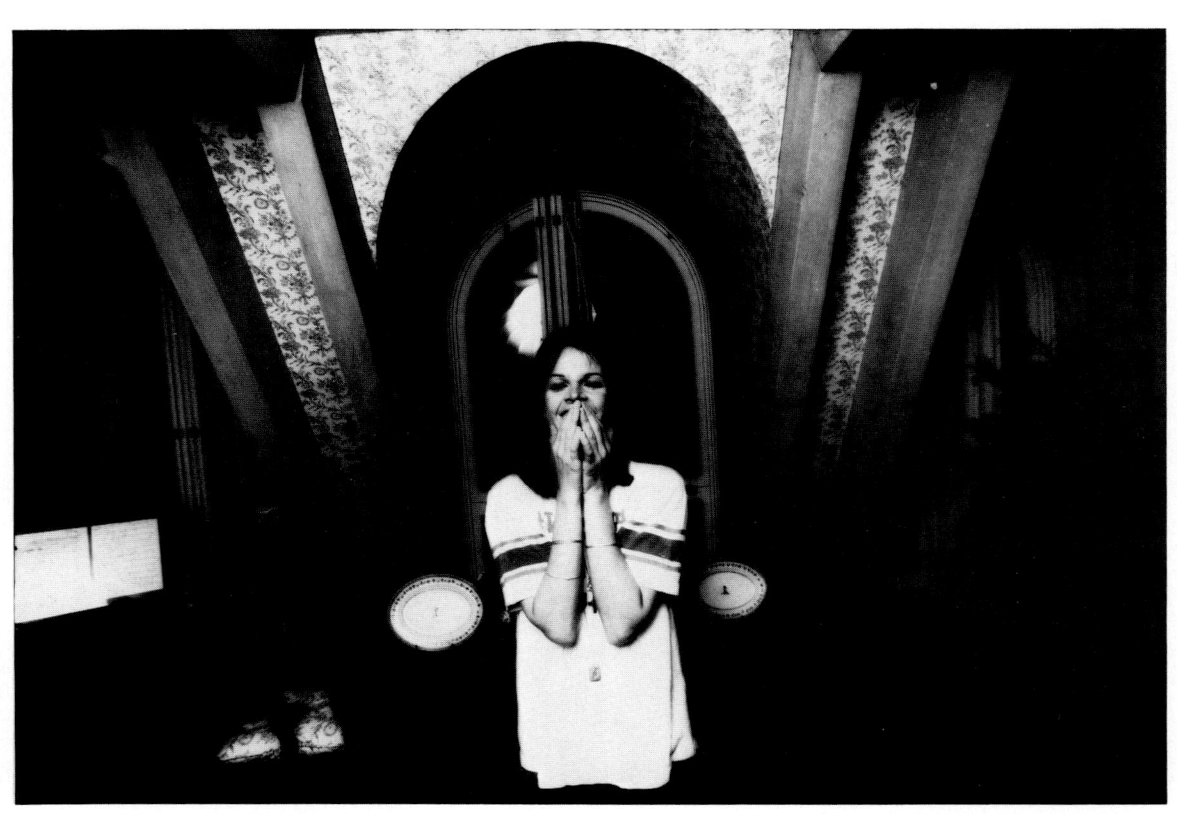

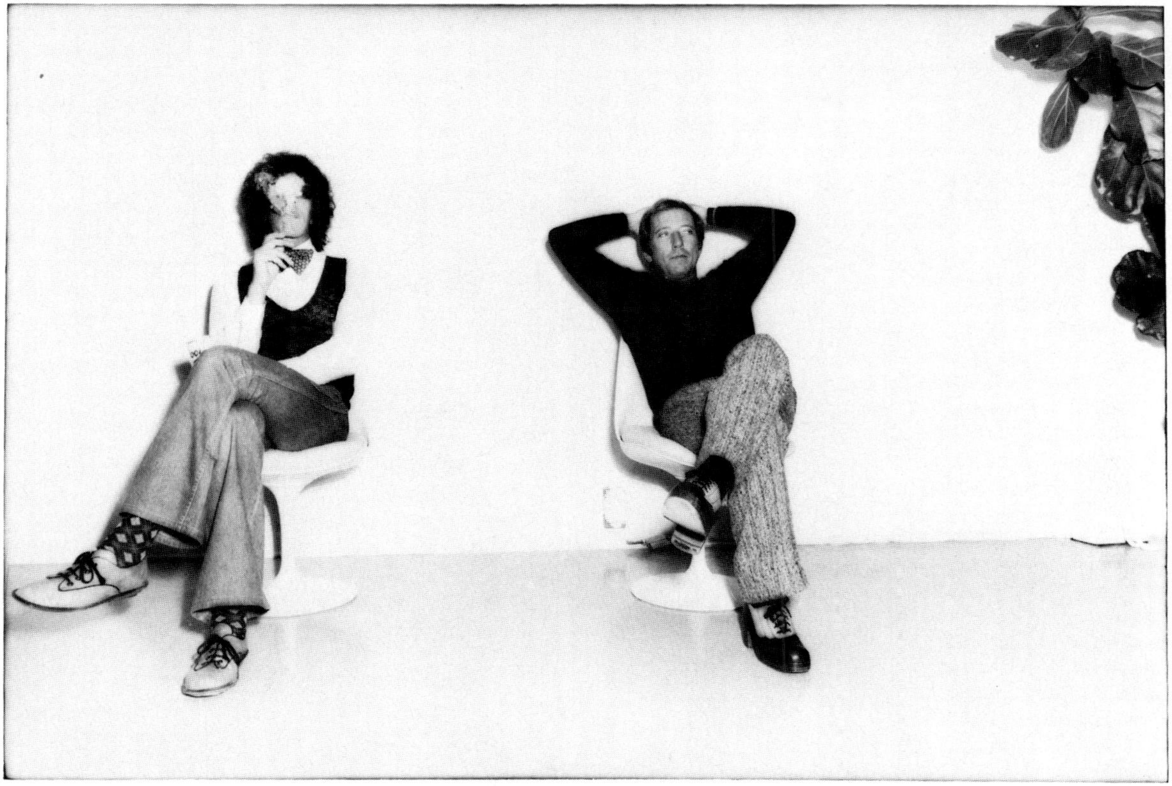

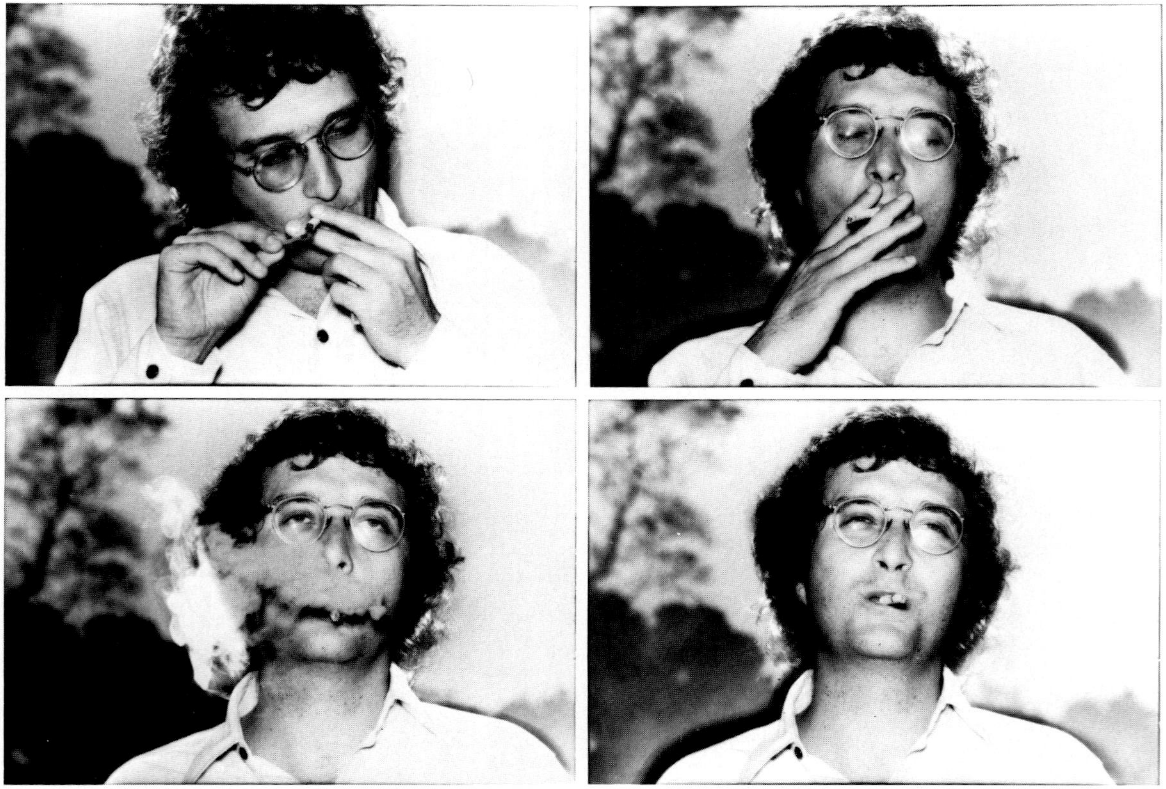

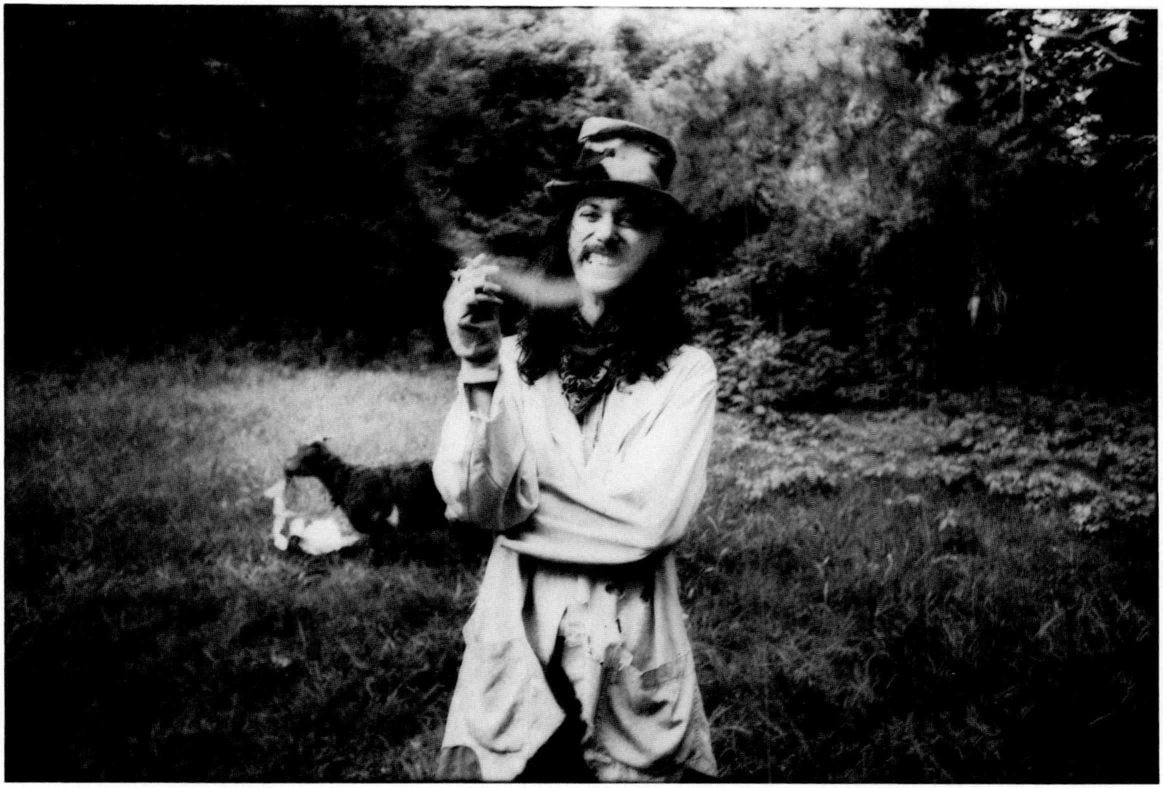

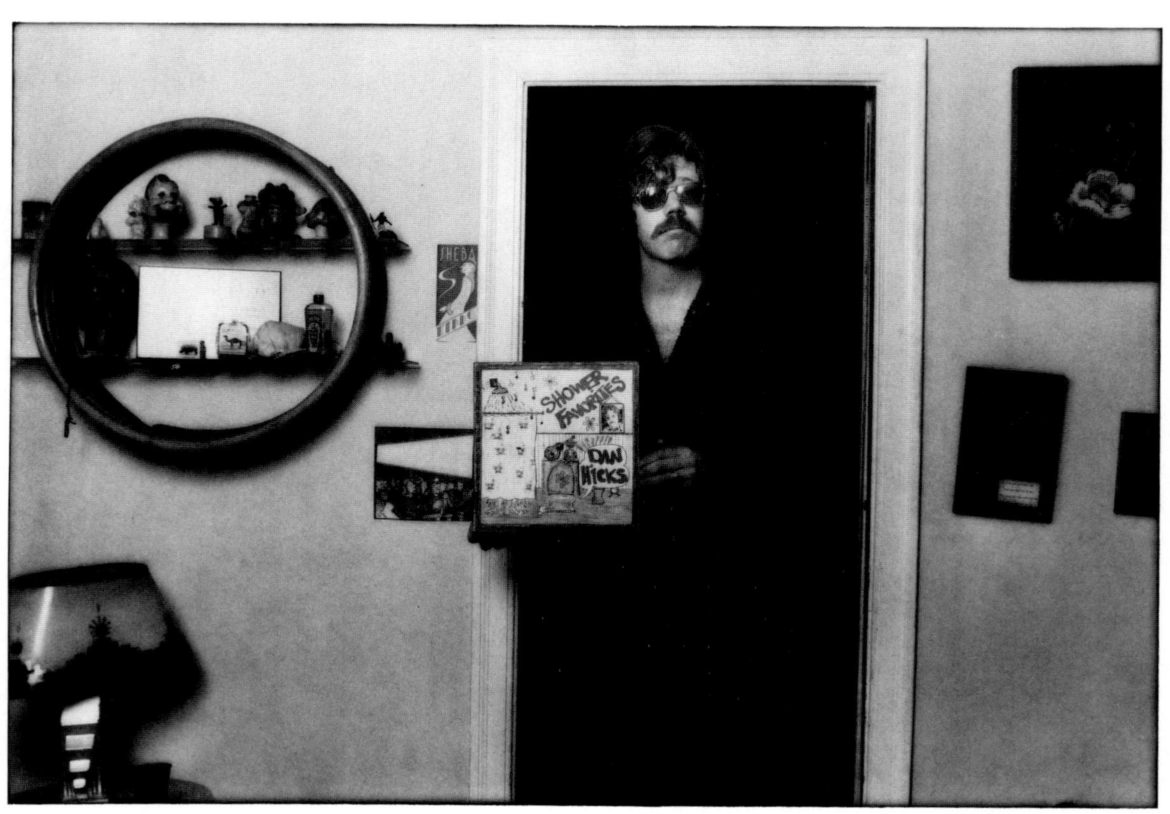
SHEBA
SHOWER FAVORITES
DAN HICKS

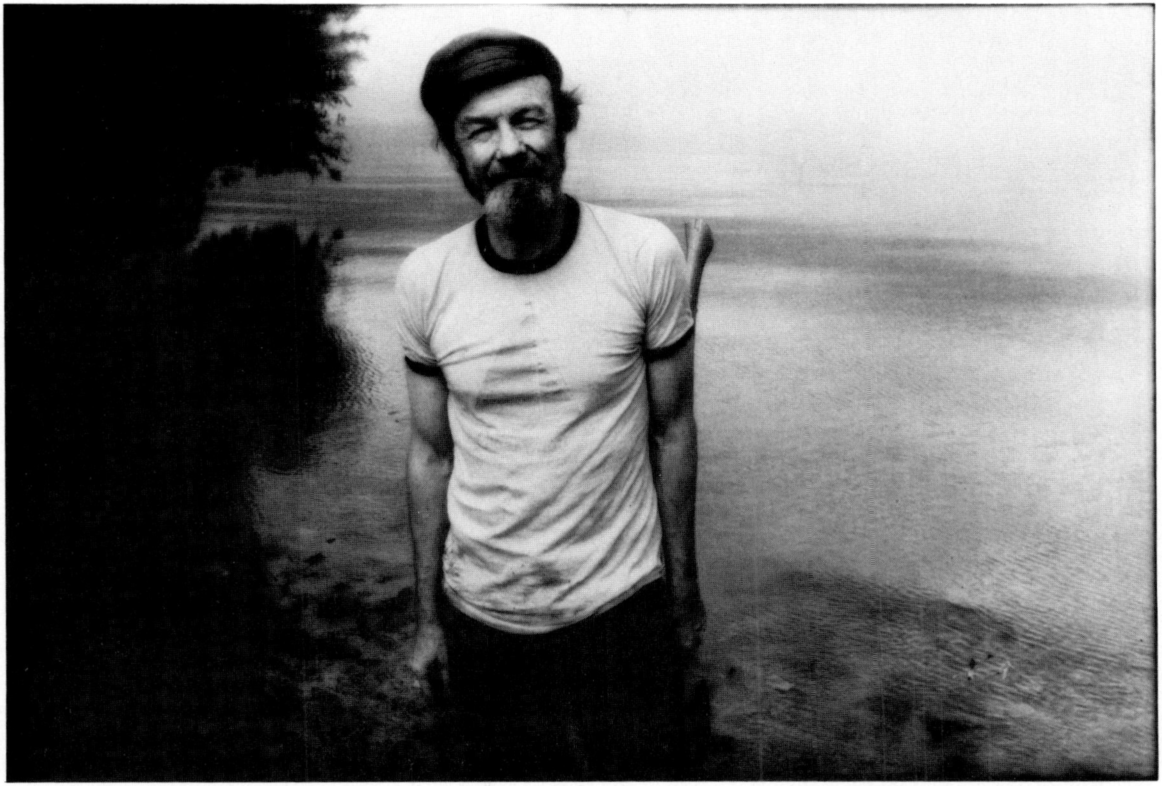

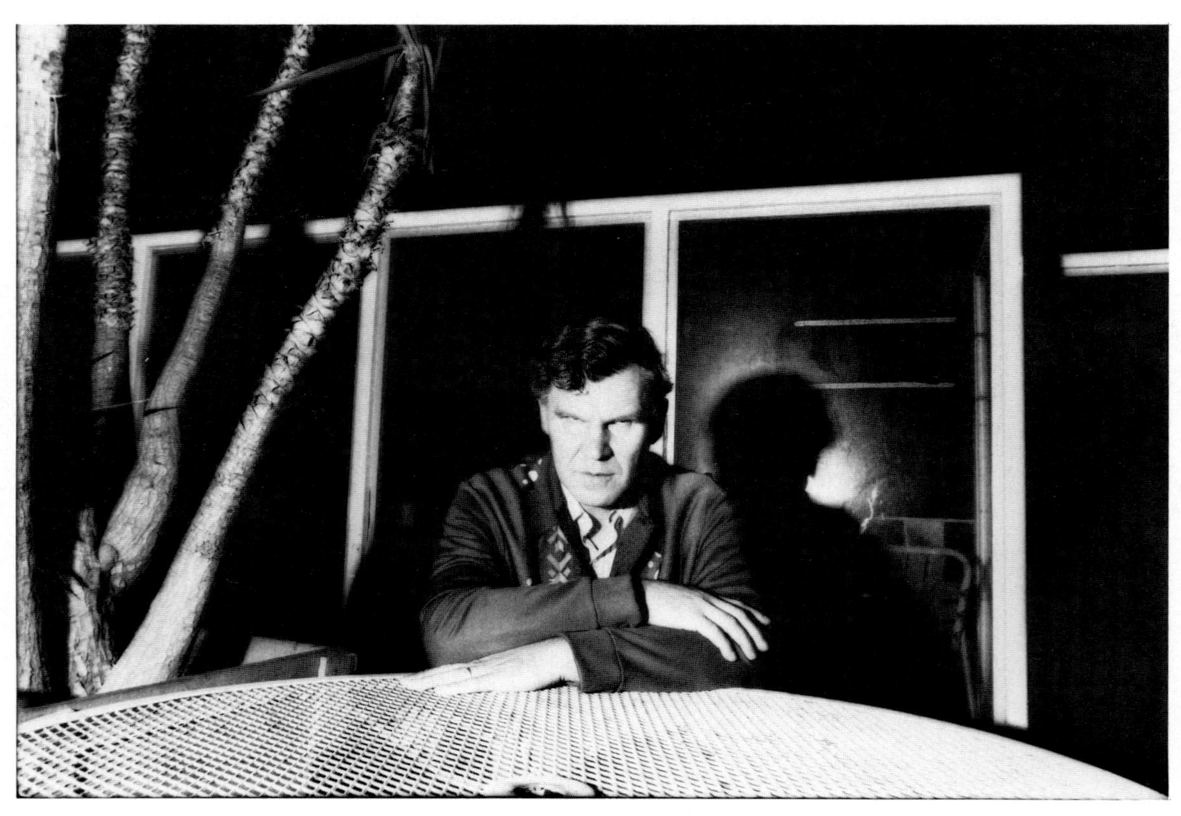

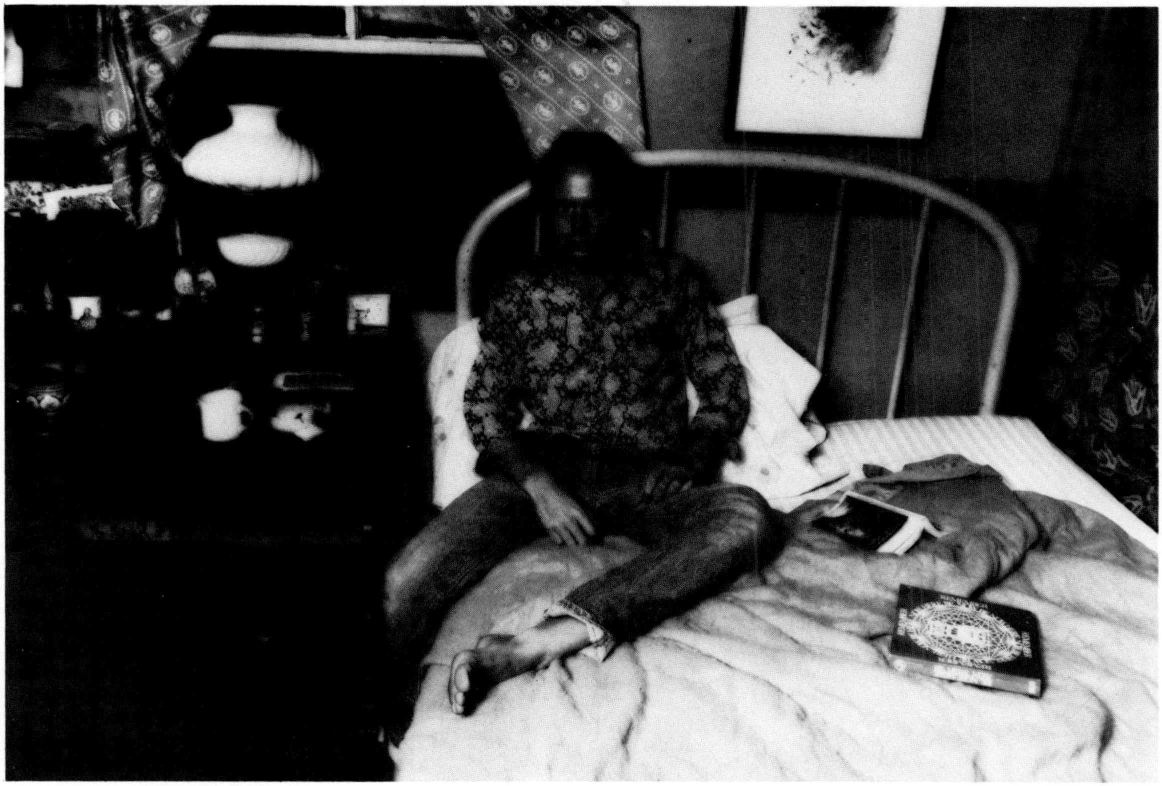

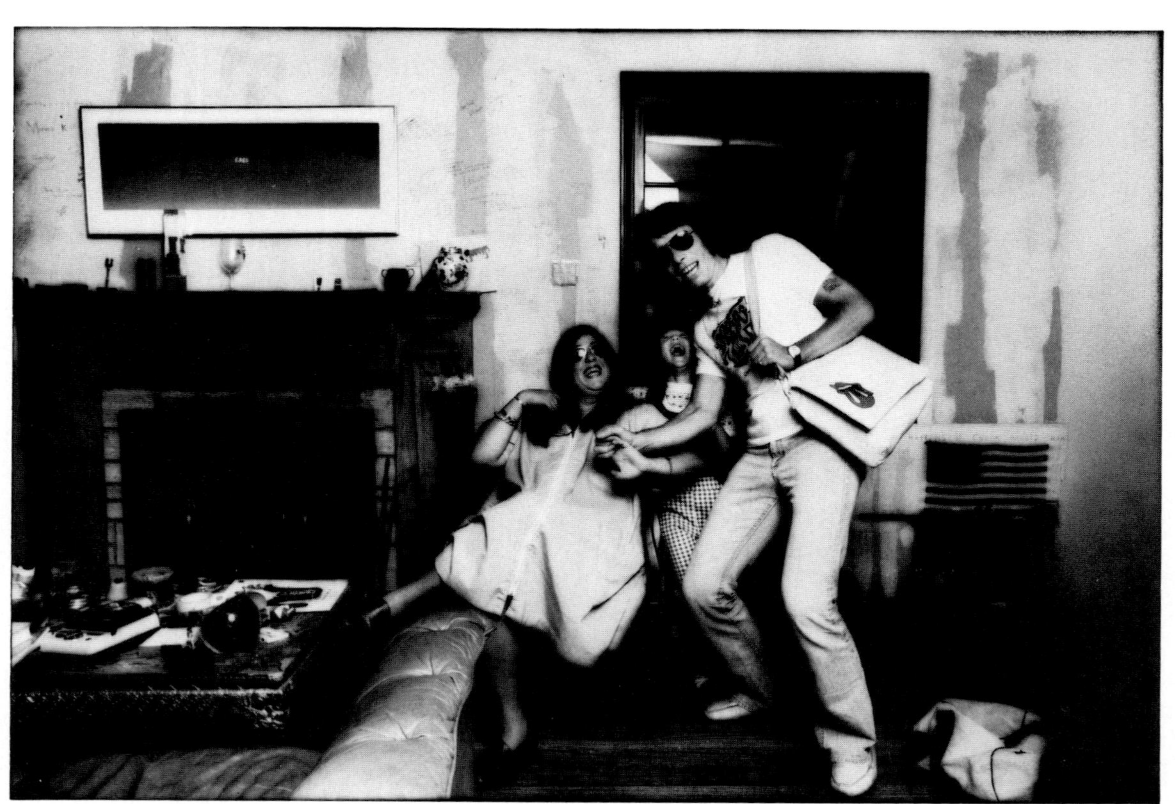

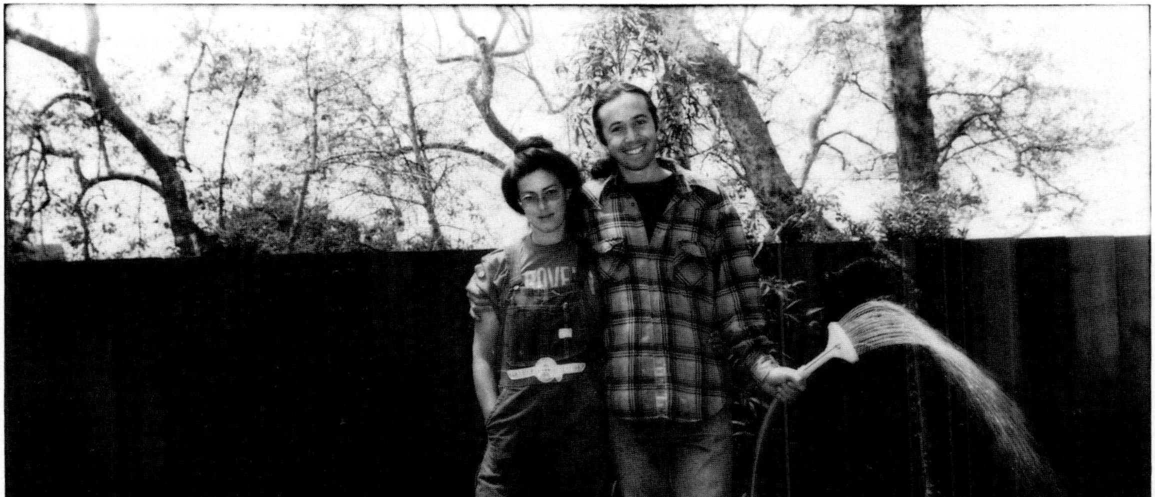

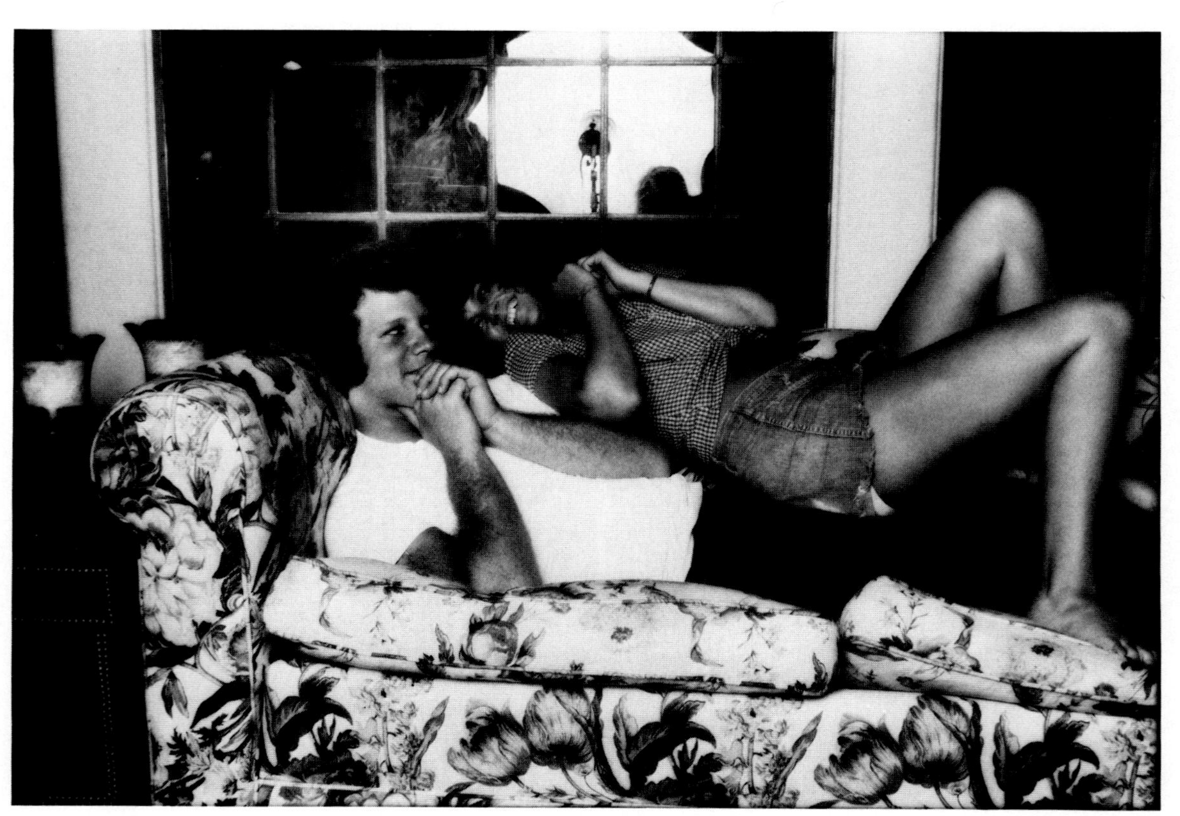

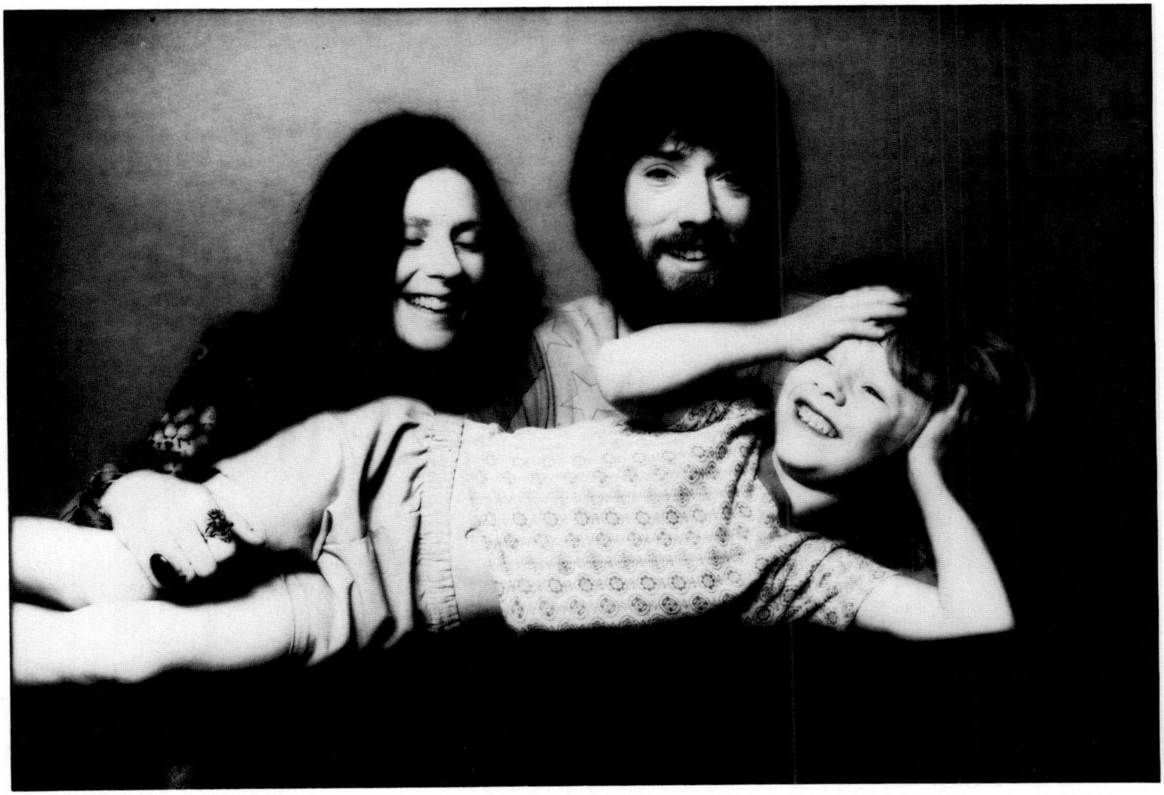

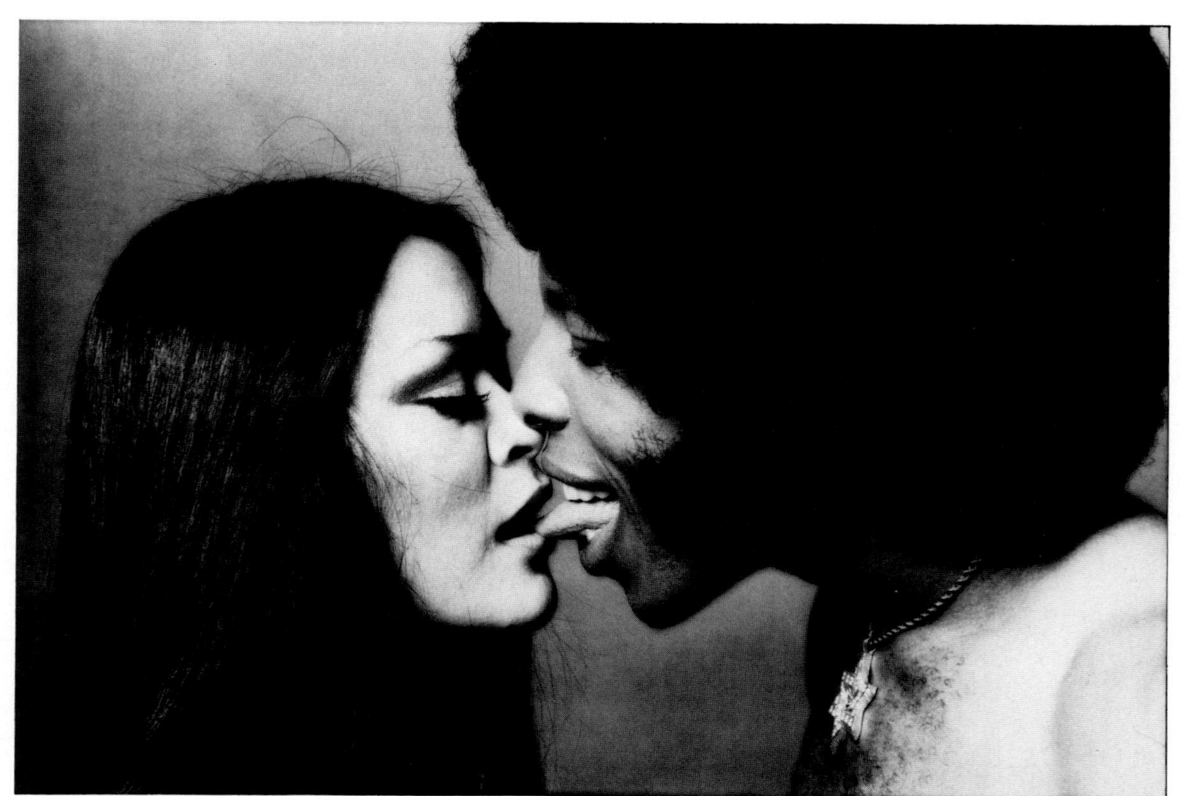

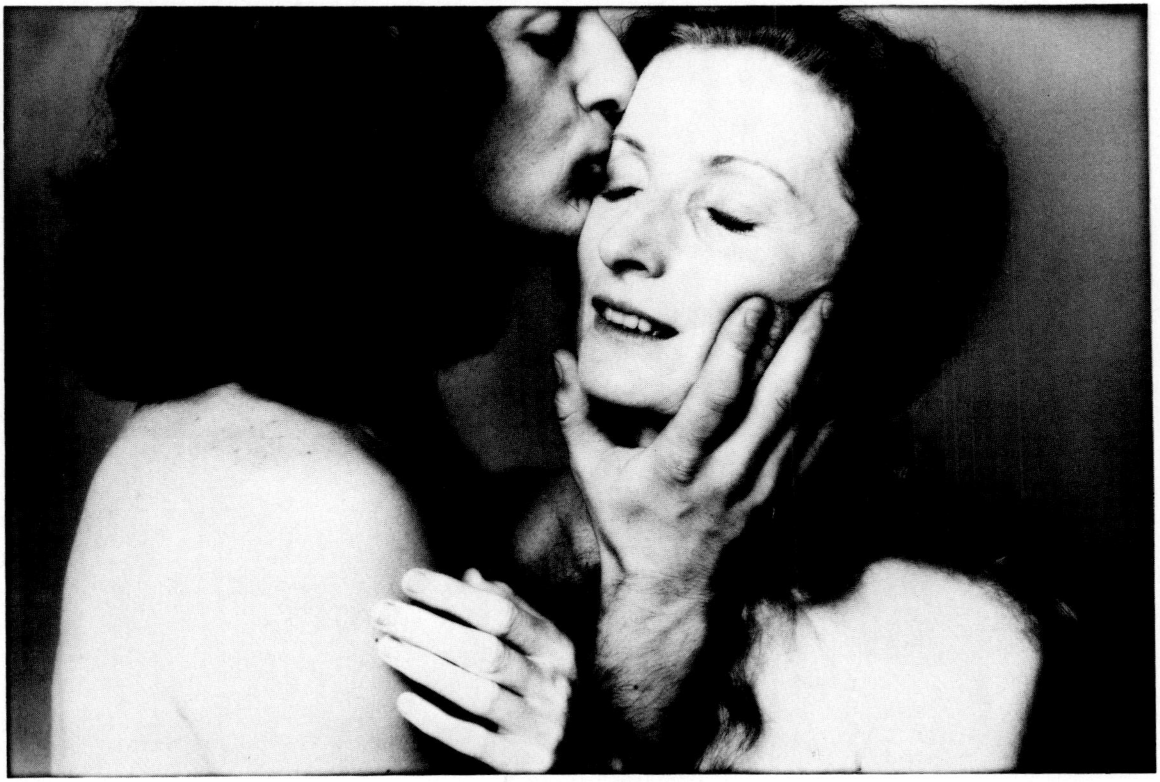

76

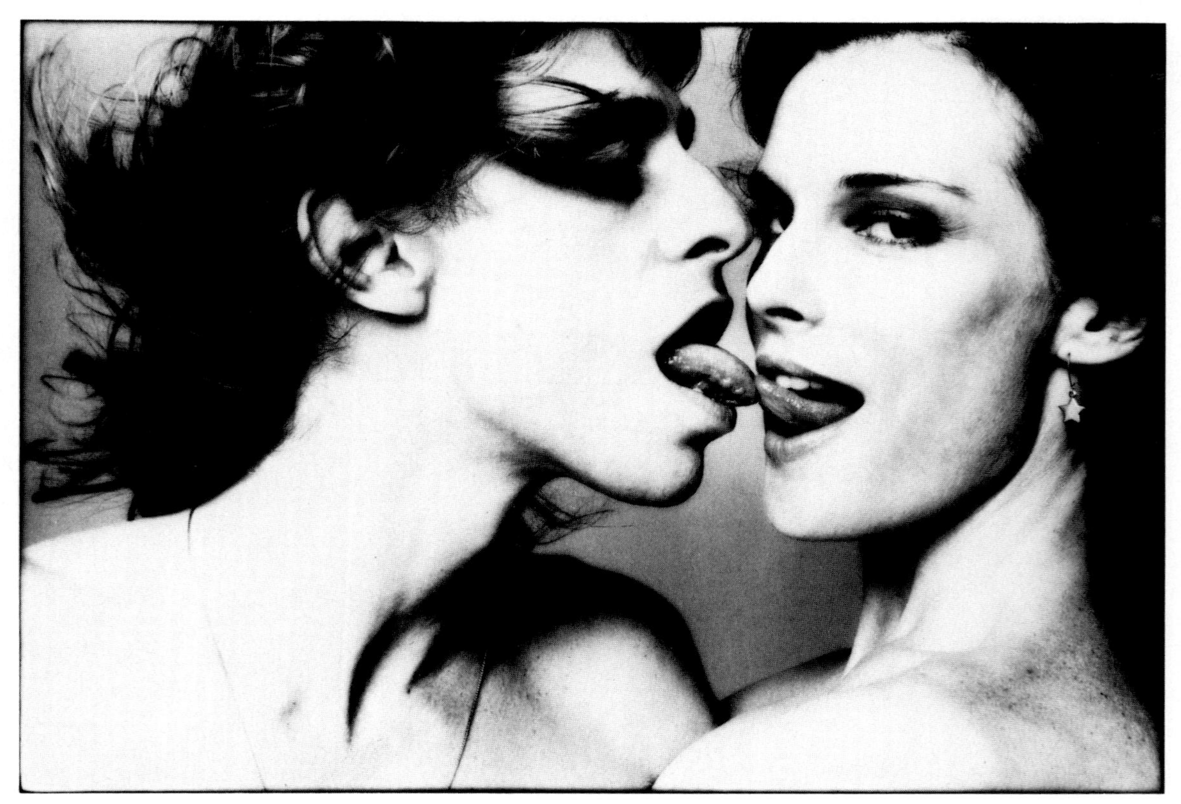

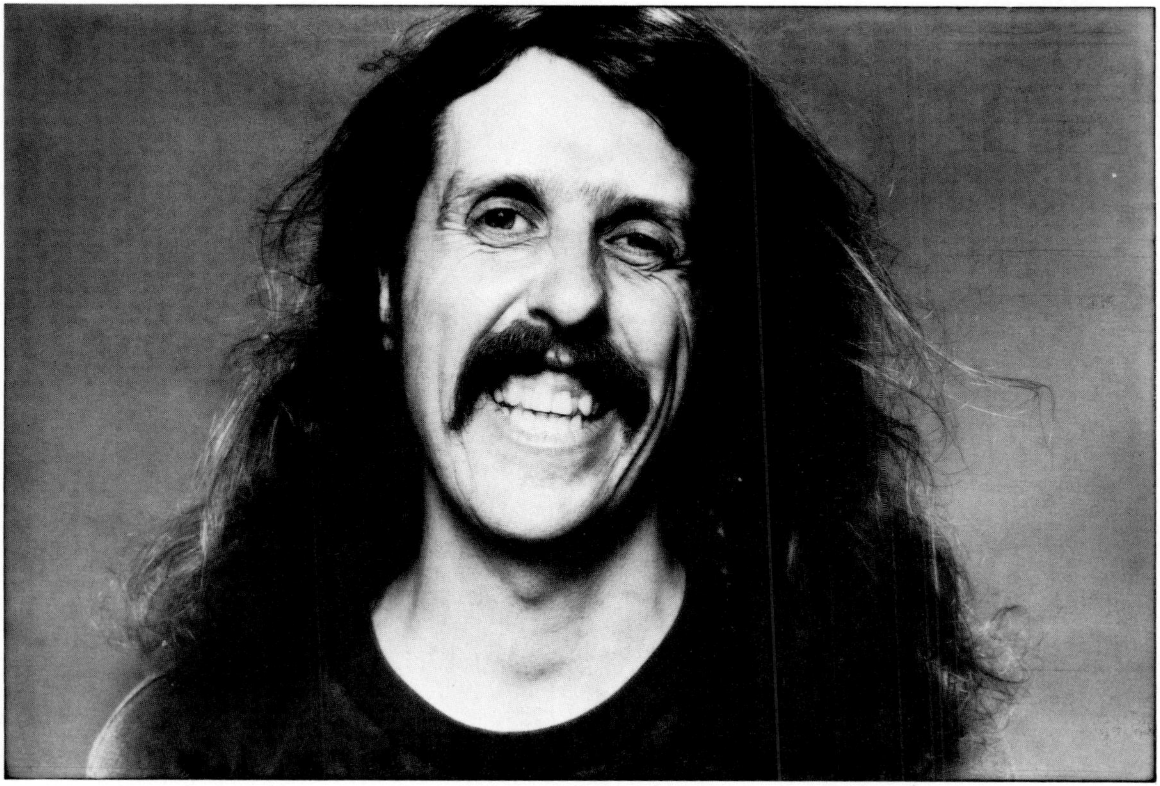

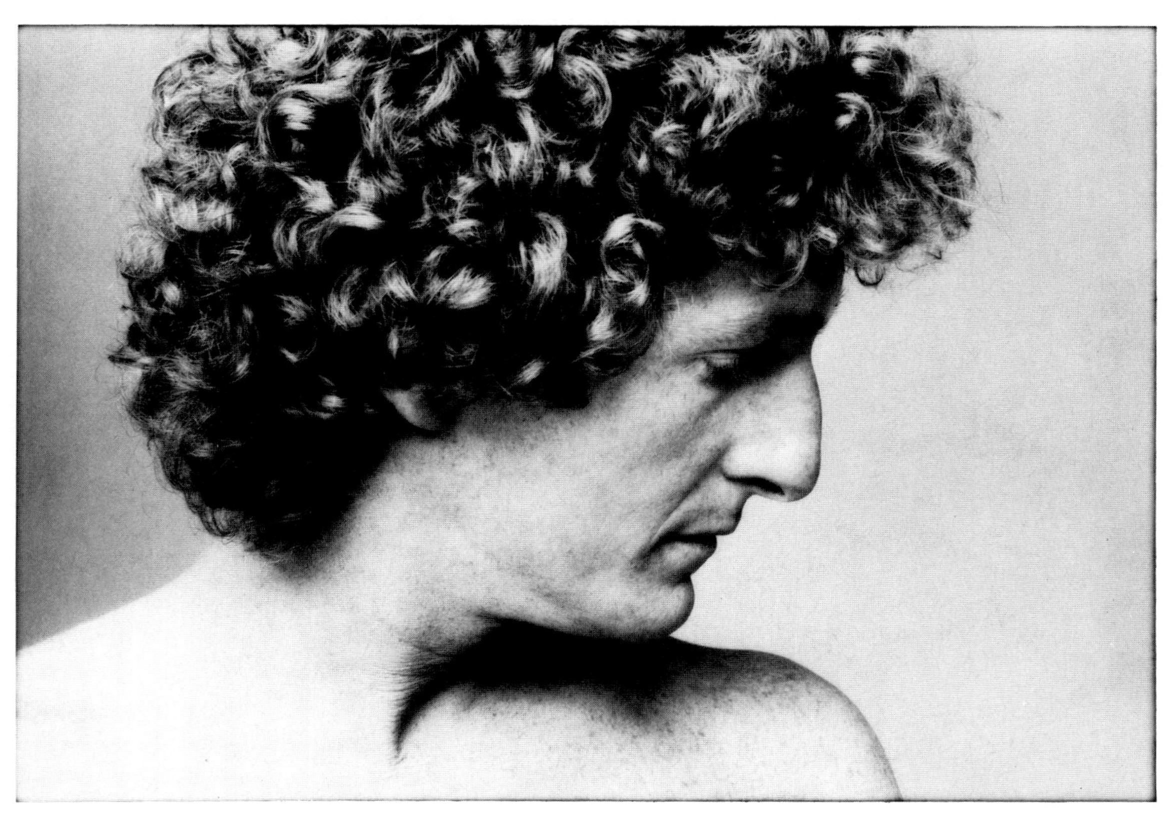

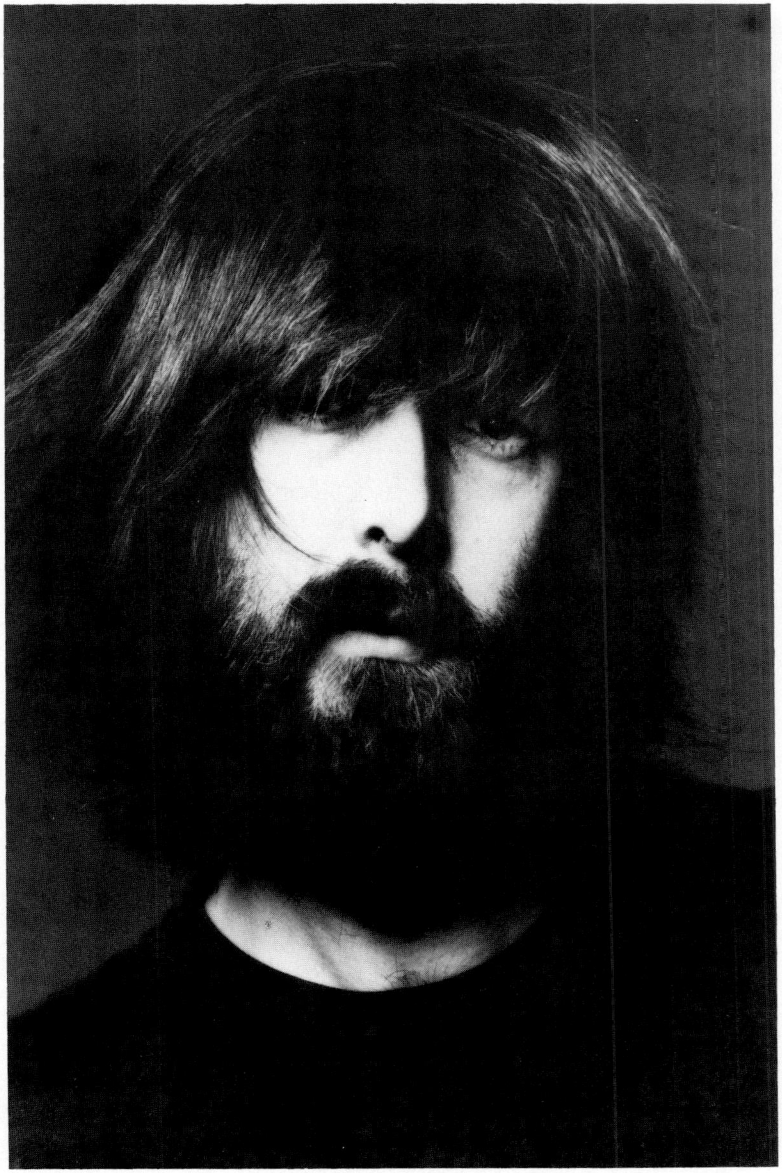

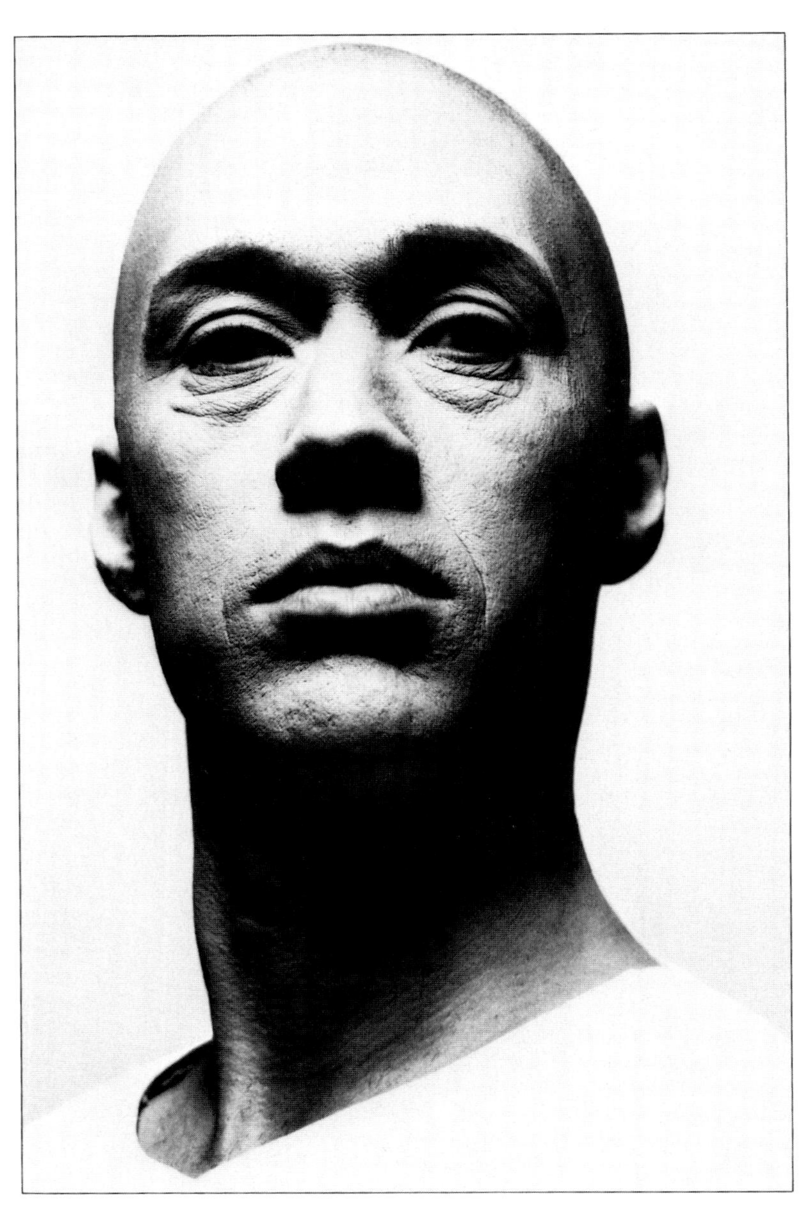

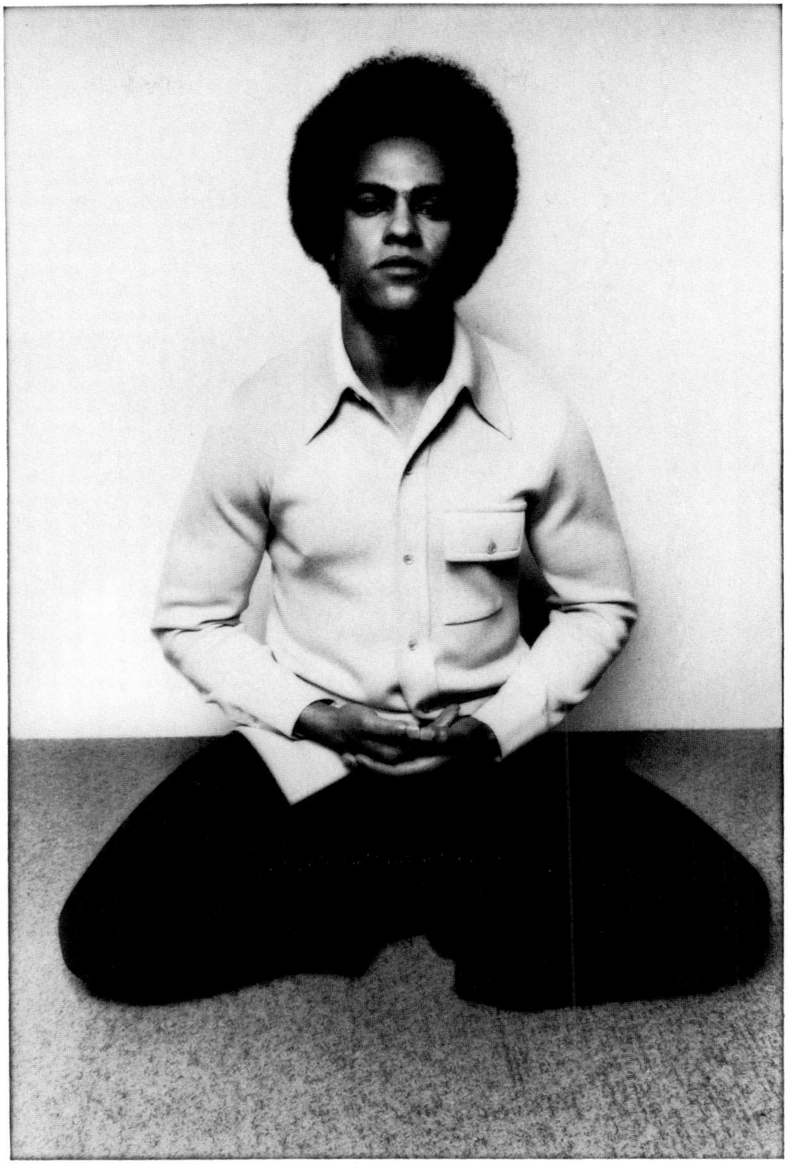

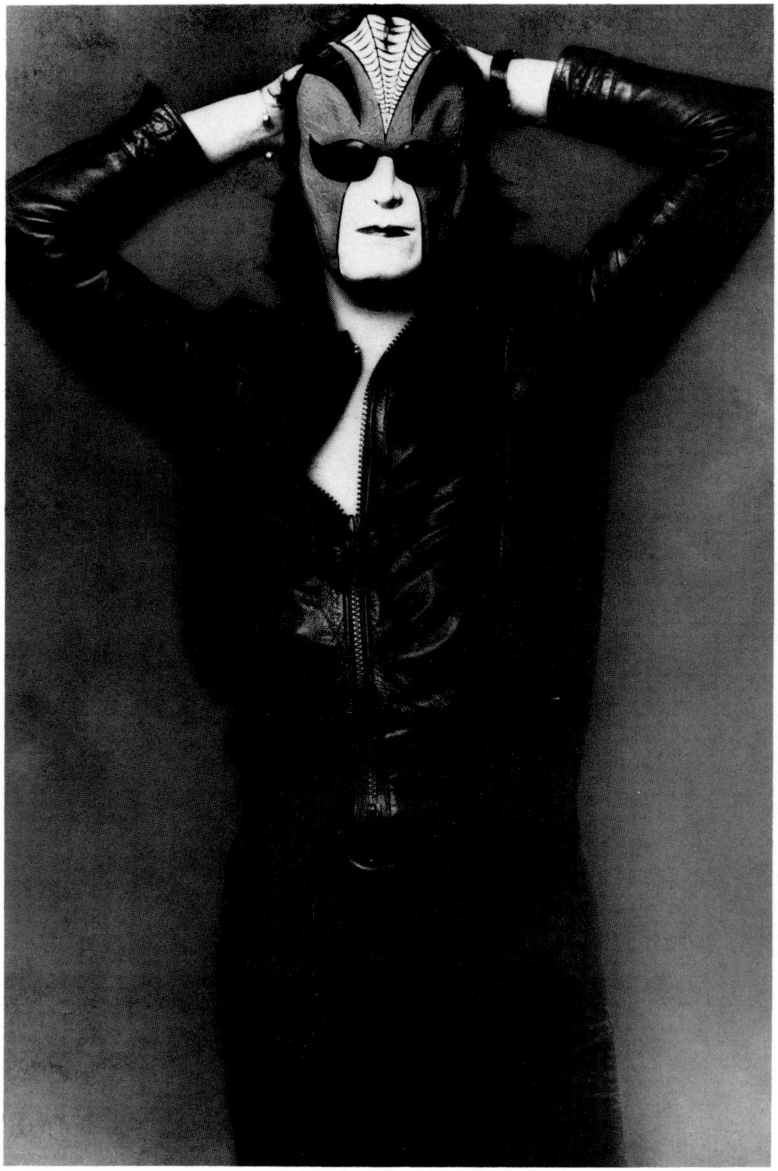

84

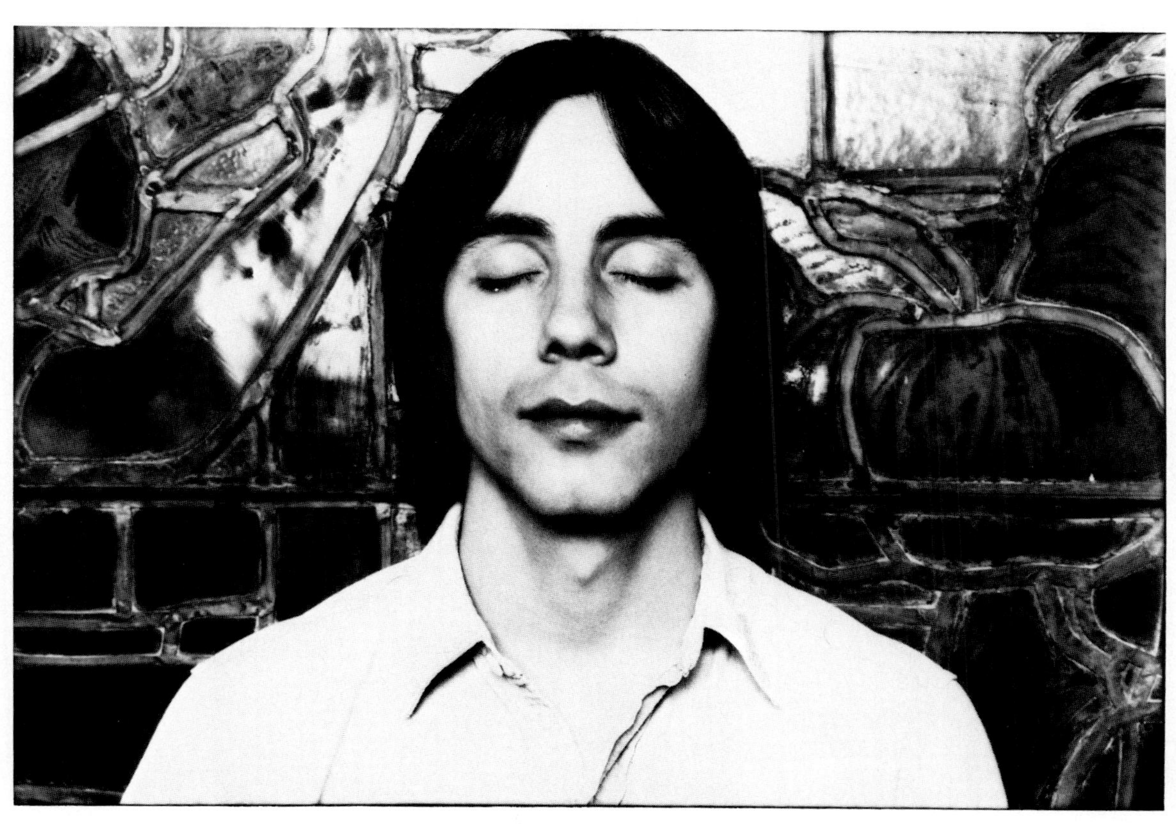

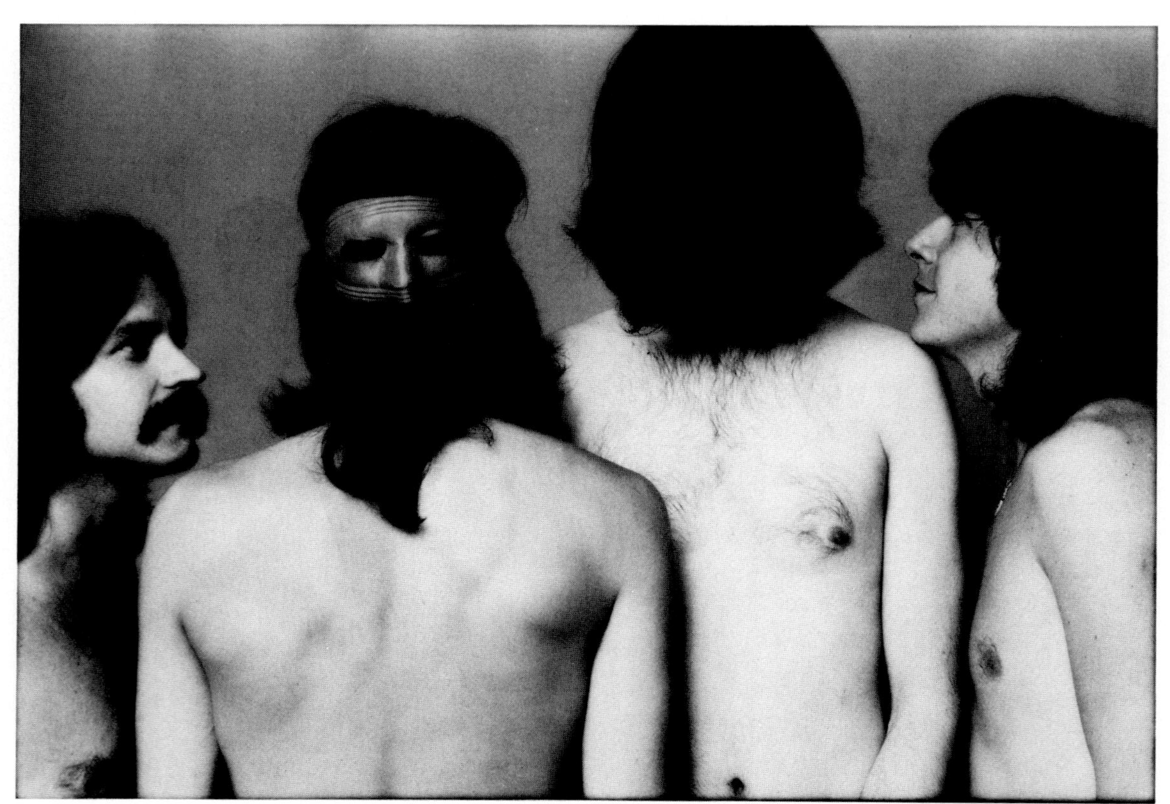

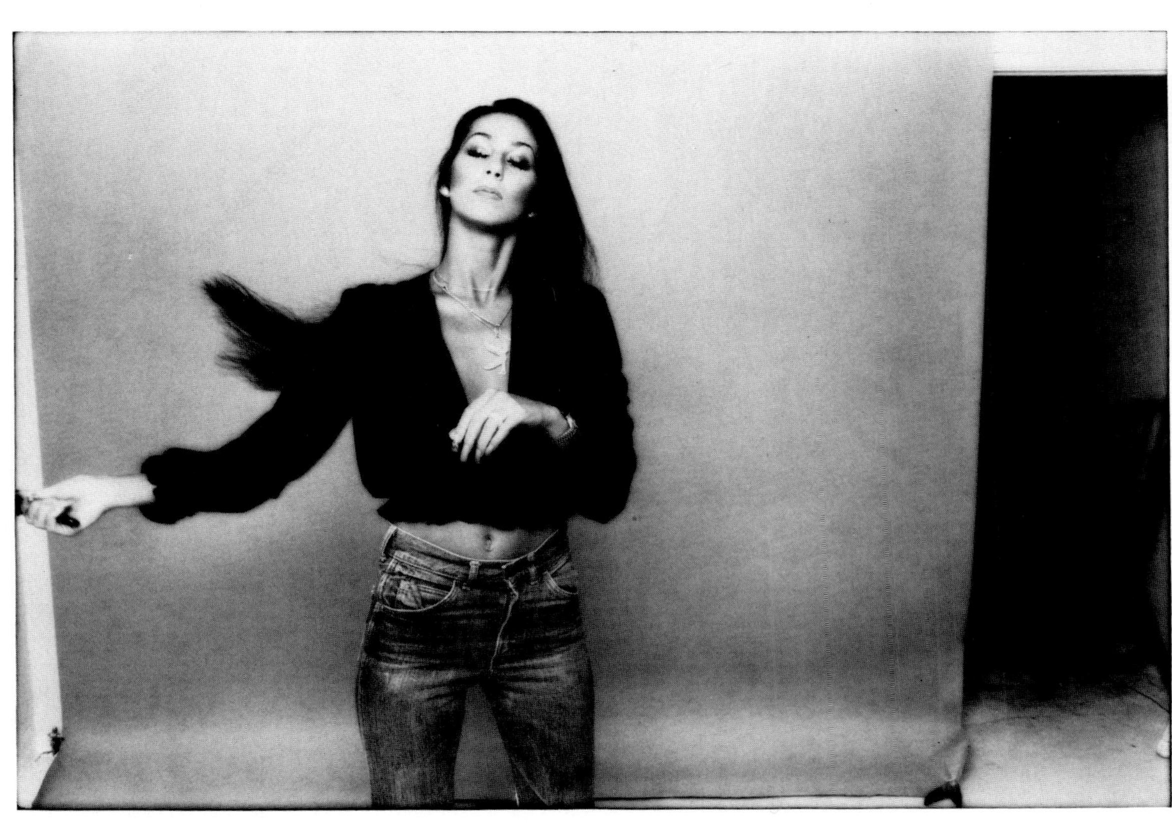

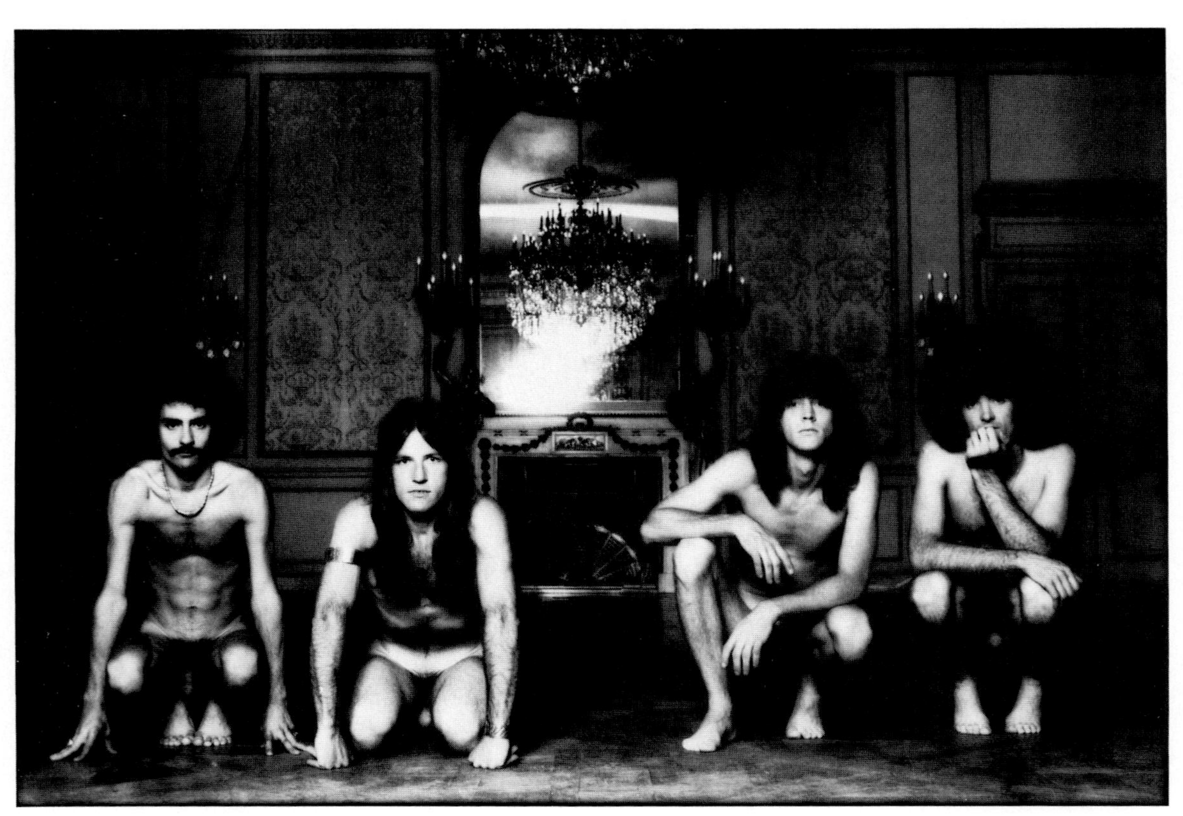

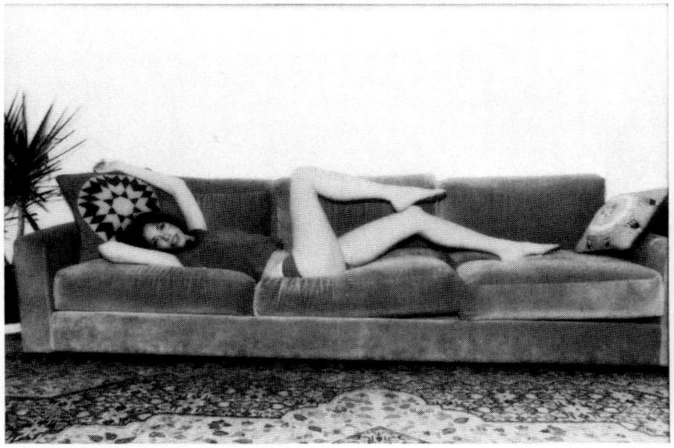

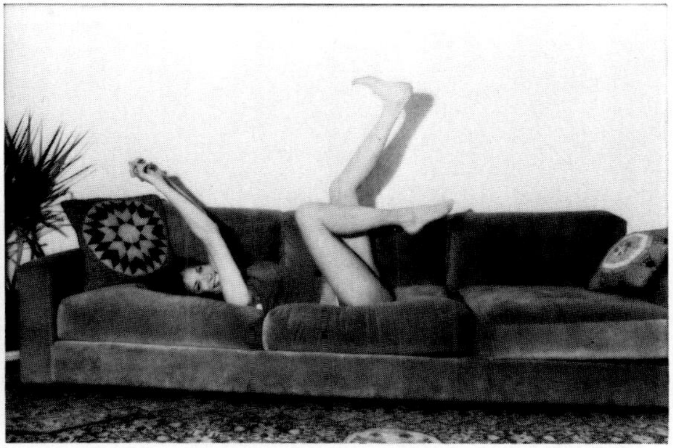

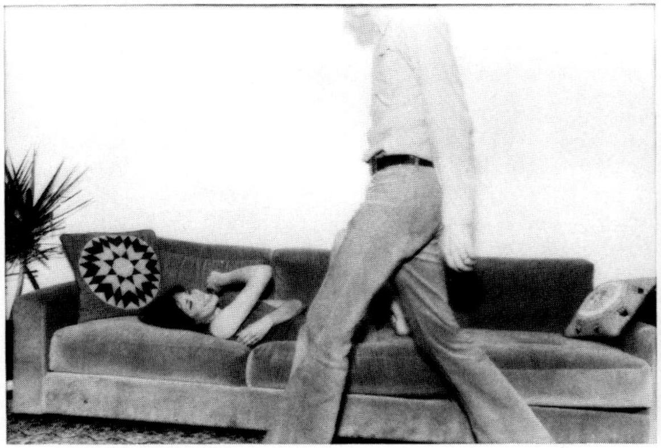

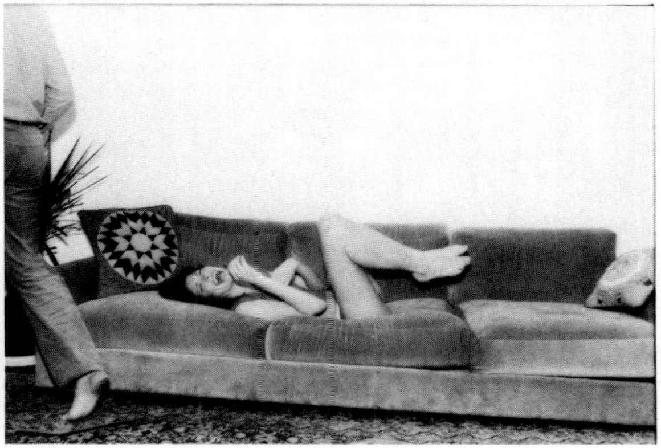

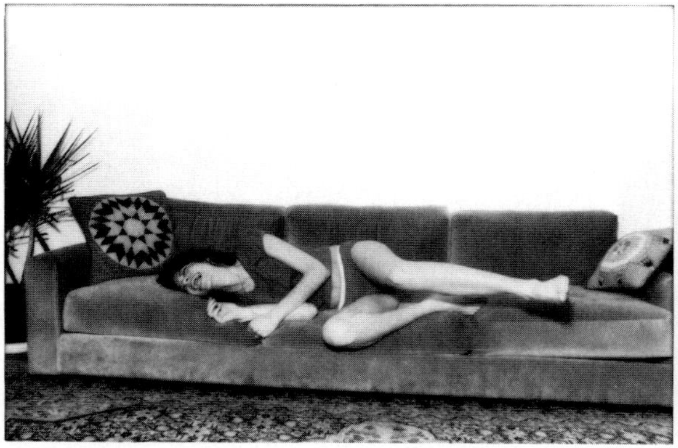

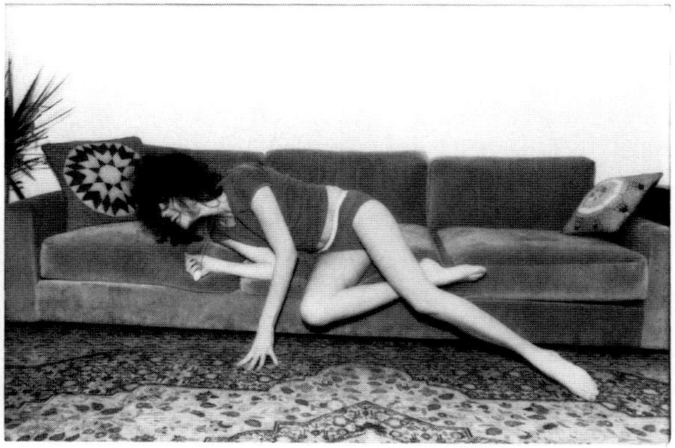

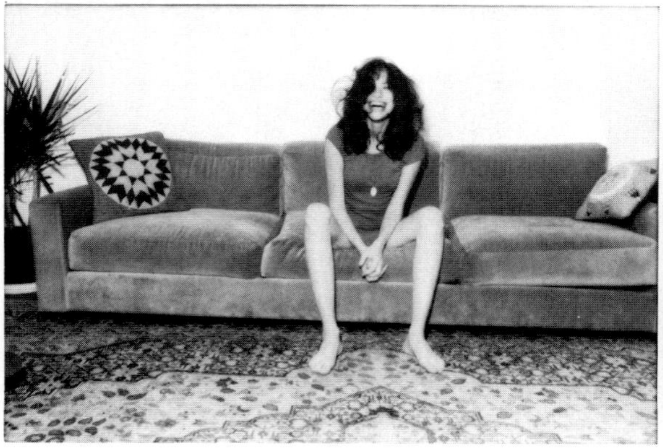

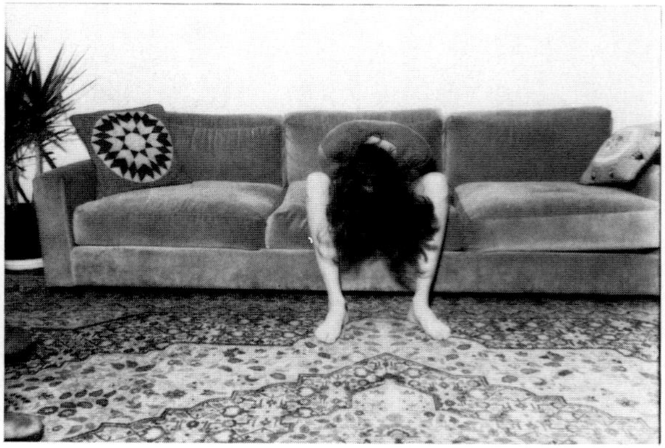

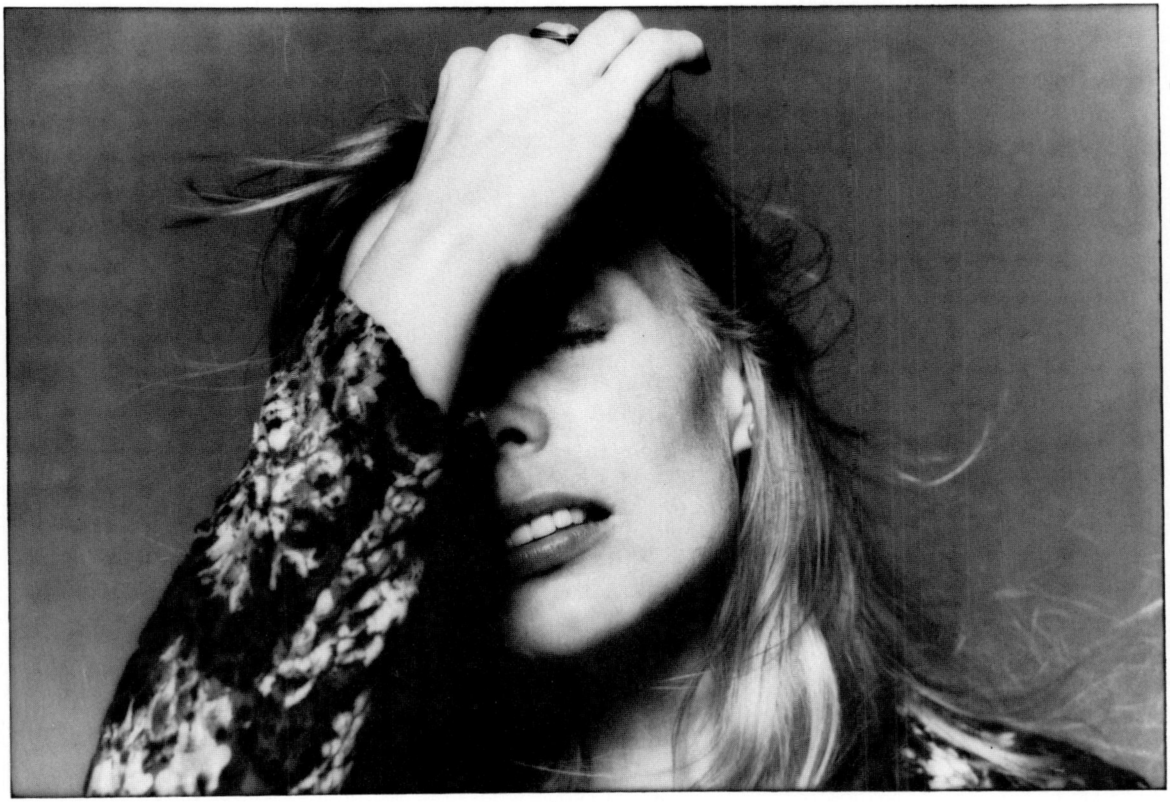

Cover. Sly Stone 1. The Band 2. Phil, Don Everly 3. J. D. Souther 4. Seals and Crofts 5. Blood, Sweat and Tears 6. Montrose 7. Mick Jagger 8. Focus 9. Andy Warhol 10. Helen Reddy 11. Claudia Lennear 12. Mott the Hoople 13. Cheyenne 14, 15. Rolling Stones 16. Barry White 17. Keith Richard 18. John Lee Hooker 19. Vassar Clements 20. Ira Friedlander 21. Frank Zappa 22. Stevie Wonder 23. Miles Davis 24. Patti Smith, Robert Mapplethorpe 25. James Taylor 26. Roger McGuinn 27. Bill Withers 28. Isaac Hayes 29. Bobby Womack 30. Ike, Tina Turner 31. Sonny Terry, Brownie McGhee 32. B. B. King 33. Furry Lewis 34. Mike Bloomfield 35. John Mayall 36. Buffy Sainte-Marie 37. Zolar X 38. Lynda Hoxit, Al Kooper 39. Lynda Hoxit 40. Lori Lieberman 41. Roy Wood 42. Tim Buckley 43. Sami Jo 44. Todd Rundgren 45. Leo Kottke 46. Denny Doherty 47. Edgar Winter 48. Brewer and Shipley 49. Sam and Dave 50, 51. Steve Martin 52. Roger Calloway 53. Johnny Winter and friends 54. The Monkees 55. Pointer Sisters 56. Bloodstone 57. Sha Na Na 58. Graham Central Station 59. Sleepy John Estes 60. Bob Hite 61. Alice Cooper 62. Buck Wilkin 63. Claudine Longet 64. Richard Perry, Andy Williams 65. Randy Newman 66. Jim Crosswaite 67. Dan Hicks 68. Pete Seeger 69. Doc Watson 70. George Gerdes 71. Cass, Owen Elliot, George Caldwell 72. Susan, Ry Cooder 73. Albert Brooks, Linda Ronstadt 74. Lynda, Eric, Harvey Mandel 75. Kathy, Sly Stone 76. Michel, Viva 77. Chris, Tony Clayton DeMarco 78. Chris Darrow 79. Marjoe 80. Spencer Davis 81. David Carradine 82. Huey Newton 83. Steve Miller 84. Jackson Browne 85. Nitty Gritty Dirt Band 86. Cher 87. Grand Funk 88, 89. Carly Simon, James Taylor 90. Joni Mitchell